How Can Suicide Be Reduced?

Other titles in the *In Controversy* series:

How Can Suicide Be Reduced?

Peggy J. Parks

INCONTROVERSY

ReferencePoint
Press®

San Diego, CA

For more information, contact:
ReferencePoint Press, Inc.
PO Box 27779
San Diego, CA 92198
www.ReferencePointPress.com

LIBRARY OF CONGRESS CATALOGING-IN-PUBLICATION DATA

Parks, Peggy J., 1951–
    How can suicide be reduced? / by Peggy J. Parks.
      pages cm. -- (In controversy series)
    Audience: Grade 9 to 12
    Includes bibliographical references and index.
    ISBN-13: 978-1-60152-662-5 (hardback)
    ISBN-10: 1-60152-662-8 (hardback)
  1. Suicide—Prevention—Juvenile literature. I. Title.
    HV6545.P237   2014
    362.28'6--dc23
                                                              2013046951

Contents

Foreword

I n 2008, as the US economy and economies worldwide were falling into the worst recession since the Great Depression, most Americans had difficulty comprehending the complexity, magnitude, and scope of what was happening. As is often the case with a complex, controversial issue such as this historic global economic recession, looking at the problem as a whole can be overwhelming and often does not lead to understanding. One way to better comprehend such a large issue or event is to break it into smaller parts. The intricacies of global economic recession may be difficult to understand, but one can gain insight by instead beginning with an individual contributing factor, such as the real estate market. When examined through a narrower lens, complex issues become clearer and easier to evaluate.

This is the idea behind ReferencePoint Press's *In Controversy* series. The series examines the complex, controversial issues of the day by breaking them into smaller pieces. Rather than looking at the stem cell research debate as a whole, a title would examine an important aspect of the debate such as *Is Stem Cell Research Necessary?* or *Is Embryonic Stem Cell Research Ethical?* By studying the central issues of the debate individually, researchers gain a more solid and focused understanding of the topic as a whole.

Each book in the series provides a clear, insightful discussion of the issues, integrating facts and a variety of contrasting opinions for a solid, balanced perspective. Personal accounts and direct quotes from academic and professional experts, advocacy groups, politicians, and others enhance the narrative. Sidebars add depth to the discussion by expanding on important ideas and events. For quick reference, a list of key facts concludes every chapter. Source notes, an annotated organizations list, bibliography, and index provide student researchers with additional tools for papers and class discussion.

The *In Controversy* series also challenges students to think critically about issues, to improve their problem-solving skills, and to sharpen their ability to form educated opinions. As President Barack Obama stated in a March 2009 speech, success in the twenty-first century will not be measurable merely by students' ability to "fill in a bubble on a test but whether they possess 21st century skills like problem-solving and critical thinking and entrepreneurship and creativity." Those who possess these skills will have a strong foundation for whatever lies ahead.

No one can know for certain what sort of world awaits today's students. What we can assume, however, is that those who are inquisitive about a wide range of issues; open-minded to divergent views; aware of bias and opinion; and able to reason, reflect, and reconsider will be best prepared for the future. As the international development organization Oxfam notes, "Today's young people will grow up to be the citizens of the future: but what that future holds for them is uncertain. We can be quite confident, however, that they will be faced with decisions about a wide range of issues on which people have differing, contradictory views. If they are to develop as global citizens all young people should have the opportunity to engage with these controversial issues."

In Controversy helps today's students better prepare for tomorrow. An understanding of the complex issues that drive our world and the ability to think critically about them are essential components of contributing, competing, and succeeding in the twenty-first century.

Preventable Tragedies

Before taking his own life in October 2013, twenty-six-year-old Joshua Marks had made strides toward achieving a lifelong dream. Known as a "gentle giant" because of his towering height and kind nature, Marks loved cooking and had longed to become a renowned chef. When he earned a spot on the reality TV show *MasterChef*, it looked as though his dream was within reach. But even as he was becoming a celebrity with a growing number of fans, the people closest to him knew that he was suffering. Marks had bipolar disorder, a severe mental illness that involves drastic mood shifts ranging from hyperexcitability (mania) to crushing bouts of depression. Coping with the disorder's extreme ups and downs can make life difficult and stressful for those who have it, and Marks was no exception. "Behind that huge smile," says a statement from his family, "Josh was in the battle of his life fighting mental illness."[1]

Inexplicable Despair

After filming on *MasterChef* was complete and Marks had returned home, his mother, Paulette Mitchell, could see that he was very ill and needed to be hospitalized. But as she desperately searched for an inpatient treatment program for him, she ran into one roadblock after another, including a severe shortage of psychiatric beds and the inability to find a program that would accept his insurance. This was terribly frustrating, as she explains: "How can you appropriately treat your loved one's mental health challenges if access to necessary care is virtually non-existent?"[2] Unable to find the ideal solution for her son, Mitchell enrolled him in an outpatient program, and he began to attend daily sessions. It seemed he was making progress—until some unexpected news threw him into a state of turmoil. A doctor told Marks that his mental illness was actually schizophrenia, and upon hearing that, he became agitated and distraught. "He was just coming to terms with having been diagnosed with bipolar disorder," says Mitchell, "but he just couldn't handle this new diagnosis."[3]

Mitchell was frightened for her son and vowed to stay close to him until she felt he was out of danger. On October 11, 2013, she left him alone for several hours while she ran an errand. During the short time his mother was gone, Marks left the house and was spotted by a neighbor walking through an alley carrying a gun. Mitchell was alerted to this by a call on her cell phone, and she frantically began driving through neighborhood streets in search of Marks. She found him lying on the ground, dead from a self-inflicted gunshot wound. "I screamed for help and held him," says Mitchell. "I just didn't get to my boy on time. I didn't get to my boy."[4]

"In the past, many scientists believed that suicide was a terrible side effect of other mental disorders."[7]

— National Institute of Mental Health.

Immense Challenges

When people lose a loved one to suicide, invariably the first thing they want to know is why: Why would someone believe that death is more appealing than life? Could the tragedy have been prevented? And if so, how? The heartbreaking reality for those who are left behind is that the only person who could answer such questions is gone forever. "It's hard to get inside a dead person's mind to sort the puzzle out," says journalist Brian Resnick. "The satisfying answers die with them."[5]

For US health officials, finding answers to questions about suicide is of foremost importance because the statistics are disturbing—and growing more so. According to 2012 data from the Centers for Disease Control and Prevention (CDC), 38,364 people took their own lives in 2010. This was an all-time high; for the first time ever, more people died by their own hand than were killed in motor vehicle crashes, and suicides outnumbered homicides three

Studies of the human brain, and in particular the brains of people who have committed suicide, may provide clues to understanding how a person can view death as the only option for escaping from life's problems.

to one. "This issue touches virtually every family, and certainly every neighborhood and community in this great nation," says former US senator Gordon H. Smith, whose son committed suicide in 2003. "And it is something we can do something about."[6]

Doing something about suicide—which means devising ways to prevent people from killing themselves—is an extraordinarily difficult task, largely because suicide itself is not well understood. Although a number of factors are known to increase someone's chances of committing suicide, these are only part of a much larger and more complex picture. Mental illness, for example, is known to vastly increase someone's risk of suicide, but concentrating solely on mental illness is too narrow a focus, as the National Institute of Mental Health (NIMH) explains: "In the past, many scientists believed that suicide was a terrible side effect of other mental disorders. But why is it that only a small proportion of people with depression or other mental conditions attempt suicide? A growing body of evidence suggests that there is something unique about their biology that can tip them over the edge."[7]

When experts talk about the biology of suicide, they are referring to the brain—specifically, abnormalities in either the brain's physical structure or its chemistry. Although a great deal remains unknown, scientists are convinced that the brain holds many answers to questions about suicide. They have studied the brains of hundreds of people who took their own lives, and this has yielded fruitful discoveries. Perhaps this type of research will eventually help scientists understand the dysfunctional thinking that leads someone to view death as the only option for escaping from life's problems.

Critical Areas of Focus

Along with a focus on brain research, health officials are addressing the suicide problem in the United States by analyzing groups most affected by it, such as young people. According to the CDC, suicide is the third leading cause of death for youth aged ten to twenty-four. The agency estimates that each year 157,000 youth receive medical care at emergency departments for self-inflicted injuries, and 4,600 die from suicide. As with all suicides, there are no easy answers to why young people take their own lives. Says the Youth Suicide Prevention Program: "Youth suicide is a complicated and complex issue. Sometimes the warning signs are missed so that an adolescent's death by suicide feels like it has 'come out of the blue.' Sometimes the signs are ignored, preferring to believe that the young person could not be thinking about ending his/her life. And with a suicide there are often many unanswered questions—particularly why did this happen and what could have been done to prevent it."[8]

Military personnel comprise another group that is a high priority for suicide prevention efforts because of what some military officials are calling a suicide epidemic. Studies have shown that despite the enactment of nine hundred prevention programs by the US Department of Defense (DoD), the

> "Sometimes the warning signs are missed so that an adolescent's death by suicide feels like it has 'come out of the blue.'"[8]
>
> — Youth Suicide Prevention Program.

number of military suicides has more than doubled since 2001. In a 2012 article secretary of the army John M. McHugh refers to the military's suicide problem as "particularly insidious." He shares his thoughts about what needs to happen to get the problem under control—and what he says is applicable not only to the military but to the overall issue of suicide prevention. He writes: "In our quest to identify new ways to intervene and ultimately prevent suicide, a better understanding of the warnings, root causes, and at-risk populations will be essential. . . . In short, we must broaden our thinking, abandon any quest for one-size-fits-all solutions, and recognize a simply reality—while we all face our own challenges, we share a common threat."[9]

Facts

- **The American Foundation for Suicide Prevention says that contrary to common belief, suicide rates are highest during spring months and lowest during the winter, with the fewest number in December.**

- **According to NIMH director Thomas Insel, the highest risk factor for dying from suicide is having made a past attempt.**

- **Since San Francisco's Golden Gate Bridge opened in May 1937, more than 1,550 people are known to have committed suicide by leaping from it.**

How Did Suicide Prevention Become an Issue of Concern?

Throughout history, documented accounts of people who ended their lives by committing suicide have appeared in medical literature. But it was not until the twentieth century that serious consideration was given to the concept of suicide prevention. Until that time the very idea was considered outlandish, as author George Howe Colt explains in his book *November of the Soul: The Enigma of Suicide*: "At the turn of the century many physicians, in fact, refused to treat suicidal people, who were believed to be insane or doomed to suicide by heredity; suicide was a crime and a sin, and the medical profession did not wish to contaminate itself with such cases. Suicidal people were scorned, ignored, or locked up in mental hospitals."[10] One of the first people to speak out against such discrimination was a Baptist minister named Harry Marsh Warren. In 1906, after losing the chance to save a young suicidal woman, he dedicated his life to helping people who felt they no longer had any reason to live.

The Save-a-Life League

At the time Warren was serving as pastor of New York City's Central Park Baptist Church. He was also the leader of a community outreach endeavor that he called the Parish of All Strangers, which involved conducting Sunday evening religious services in the lobbies of leading hotels. Warren became a familiar figure to hotel personnel throughout the city, whom he encouraged to contact him at any time of the day or night if a hotel guest had a crisis. In his book Colt tells of such a crisis that occurred in 1906 and profoundly changed Warren's life. A young woman staying at a New York City hotel asked the manager if he could put her in touch with a minister. The manager tried to reach Warren but was unable to do so. In the meantime the woman, filled with despair and bereft of hope, took poison in an attempt to end her life.

The next morning the woman was found unconscious with an empty bottle marked *Poison* nearby. She was rushed to a hospital, and as soon as Warren heard about her plight he hurried to her bedside. The woman was able to talk to him and explain that she had become so despondent over a failed relationship that she decided she no longer wanted to live. Since no one in New York City knew her, she had traveled there from the West Coast for the sole purpose of committing suicide. She said to Warren: "I think maybe if I had talked to someone like you, I wouldn't have done it."[11] She died shortly afterward.

Warren was distraught over the young woman's death. He felt certain that he could have saved her if he had been able to talk to her before she took the poison. During his next sermon he wept openly while telling her tragic story. He went on to share his firm belief that nearly every suicide could be prevented by a combination of intelligent counsel, sympathetic understanding, and spiritual guidance. Warren concluded by encouraging anyone who had thought about suicide to write him or visit him in person. "I wish," he said, "that all who believe death is the only solution for their problems would give me a chance to prove them wrong."[12]

"I wish that all who believe death is the only solution for their problems would give me a chance to prove them wrong."[12]

— The late Harry Marsh Warren, a Baptist minister who was the first to address the issue of suicide prevention during the early twentieth century.

Before the twentieth century, people who were considered a suicide risk were often locked up in mental hospitals. Many people viewed suicide as a crime, or at the very least, a sign of insanity.

Warren's message was highly unusual because, at the time, interfering with anyone who was suicidal was unheard of. But people responded. The following morning several newspapers carried his story, and by that night about a dozen visitors had gone to see him. As he had promised, he listened to them and offered counsel, reassurance, and guidance, and he was delighted to learn later that none had gone on to commit suicide. Word began to spread throughout the city, and soon people were arriving at Warren's door every day, as Colt writes: "They were treated with what Warren described as 'human sympathy and understanding' by himself or one of several volunteers. While one-third of the cases required more than that and were referred to psychiatrists, Warren found that by merely giving troubled people a chance to talk confidentially to a stranger, he could help them get through a crisis."[13] Fueled by passion for being able to save lives, Warren decided to dedicate his life to preventing suicide. The Parish of All Strangers became the first organized suicide prevention group in US history, and in 1916 it was renamed the Save-a-Life League.

Taming the "Suicide Wave"

By 1921 Warren's group was assisting suicidal people from not only the United States but also other countries. As stated in an August 1921 *New York Times* article: "The Save-a-Life League has received thousands of letters from different parts of the world telling of sor-

---

A Philosopher's Philosophy About Suicide

François-Marie Arouet, more commonly known by his pen name Voltaire, was an eighteenth-century writer, philosopher, and political analyst from Paris, France. A powerful figure during Europe's Age of Enlightenment, Voltaire was well known for his writings on a wide variety of topics from free trade and civil liberties to social reform. In his 1764 publication *Dictionnaire philosophique* (*Philosophical Dictionary*) he discussed suicide. Referring to prominent Romans such as Brutus, Cato, and Mark Antony, Voltaire said they ended their lives because they "preferred a voluntary death to a life which they believed to be ignominious." In other words, the men felt they would be better off dying by their own hands than suffering through the humiliation and disgrace they faced in life.

Voltaire had a different perspective on suicide by common individuals, who he believed should be able to solve their problems without resorting to killing themselves. He then made reference to a concept that is still widely accepted today: Rather than acting impulsively, if suicidal people take some time to think about what they are doing, they will likely choose not to die. Voltaire wrote: "The man who, in a fit of melancholy, kills himself today would have wished to live had he waited a week."

Voltaire, "Cato. On Suicide, and the Abbe St. Cyran's Book Legitimating Suicide," *Dictionnaire philosophique* (*Philosophical Dictionary*), 1764, from University of Adelaide Ebooks. http://ebooks.adelaide.edu.au.

rows beyond human endurance, and begging for any possible help. Quantities of inspirational free literature, which the league publishes, have been sent out. At the headquarters hundreds and thousands have come either for personal help or in behalf of others."[14] Yet as dedicated as the Save-a-Life League was to its mission, it was impossible for the organization to address the rapidly growing suicide problem on its own. The same *New York Times* article refers to a "suicide wave"[15] that was sweeping across the United States, with 6,509 suicides reported to the league during the first six months of 1921.

Every one of these deaths was disturbing to Warren, but he was especially heartsick that 507 children were among the suicides—and that number had grown substantially since the previous year. In the *Times* article he issues a plea to parents, teachers, and clergy to help end the tragic childhood suicides. In an effort to increase support for his organization's work, Warren implores philanthropists and other supporters "to become members of this league and thus help us save thousands of lives annually. The need was never so great as at the present time."[16] During the 1920s and 1930s the Save-a-Life League continued to serve people in crisis, and Warren remained as committed as ever to the cause. He frequently expressed his unwavering belief that with very few exceptions, suicide was preventable, saying that he was certain of that because of his own personal experience.

> "Prior to the 1950s, except for the efforts of a few courageous practitioners, suicide went untreated as a mental health problem and was hardly ever discussed."[17]
>
> — Calvin J. Frederick, a psychologist from Encino, California.

After leading the Save-a-Life League for thirty-four years, Warren died in December 1940 at the age of seventy-nine. His son assumed the role of president and worked to keep the organization going over the following years, but this was challenging. Despite the league's decades of work and the thousands of lives that had been saved because of it, society's overall perception of suicide had not really changed. People who had attempted to take their own lives were still viewed with disdain rather than compassion, and suicide prevention efforts were not typically considered a priority even among physicians, psychologists, and members of the clergy. "Prior to the 1950s," says psychologist Calvin J. Frederick, "except for the efforts of a few courageous practitioners, suicide went untreated as a mental health problem and was hardly ever discussed. It was rarely a point of focus in the media, or in professional literature, though suicide has claimed consistently more victims than homicide."[17]

The Turning Point

Even as society preferred to ignore the suicide problem, it was escalating into a crisis. Mortality data from 1945 showed that at least twenty thousand Americans were dying by suicide each year in the United States, but the reasons for this remained unknown. Most people were uninterested in delving into the mystery, including California psychologist Edwin S. Shneidman. In 1949, however, his attitude changed radically, and his life's focus took a very different turn.

Shneidman was working for the Veterans Administration hospital in Brentwood, California. When asked by the director to draft condolence letters to the widows of two young veterans who had committed suicide, he decided to research the cases to learn more about the men. Shneidman visited the Los Angeles County coroner's office and discovered that its vaults held hundreds of suicide notes, which fascinated him. Journalist Thomas Curwen writes: "A clerk directed him to the ledgers of the city's dead, housed in a subterranean vault filled with dust and the smell of motor oil. What was supposed to be a two-hour visit turned into a daylong affair. The study of suicide and the more radical proposition that it could be prevented became his life's passion."[18]

From that day forward Shneidman was dedicated to understanding the complicated factors at the root of suicidal thinking. Through his research he discovered that contrary to common belief, the majority of people who killed themselves were not mentally ill. Rather, they suffered from deep, unbearable emotional pain that he termed "psychache." Shneidman elaborates on this in his book *A Commonsense Book of Death*, which was published in 2008 when he was ninety years old. "My theory of suicide can be rather simply stated," Shneidman ex-

"There is a great deal of mental pain and suffering without suicide—millions to one—but there is almost no suicide without a great deal of mental pain."[19]

— The late Edwin S. Shneidman, a psychologist who is considered one of the pioneers of suicide prevention.

Postmortem Diagnosis of an Icon

The late Edwin S. Shneidman was not only a prominent psychologist but also the developer of suicidology, which is the scientific study of suicide. One of his many accomplishments as a suicidologist was creating the psychological autopsy. This process is still used today to help confirm whether someone's death was an accident or suicide. It involves interviewing family members and friends to collect all available information about the deceased. Information is also gathered from available health care and psychiatric records, the forensic examination, and any other pertinent documents. The gathered data is then synthesized to create the final report on the person's death.

Shneidman's most celebrated case was the August 4, 1962, death of world-famous actress Marilyn Monroe. The Los Angeles County medical examiner asked Shneidman and his colleague Norman L. Farberow to investigate Monroe's death; although it had been confirmed that she died from an overdose of barbiturates, whether it was suicide was not known. In the course of conducting their interviews, Shneidman and Farberow learned that she had attempted suicide twice in the past and that she was deeply depressed before her death. After completing the psychological autopsy, they recommended that the death certificate list her death as "probable suicide."

Quoted in George Howe Colt, *The Enigma of Suicide*. New York: Touchstone, 1991, p. 297.

plains. "There is a great deal of mental pain and suffering without suicide—millions to one—but there is almost no suicide without a great deal of mental pain."[19] Shneidman was also convinced that most people who were suicidal were only in that state for a brief period of time; thus, if someone intervened early enough their lives could likely be saved.

"First-Aid" for the Troubled Mind

Shneidman's perspective about suicide prevention was shared by his colleague and fellow psychologist Norman L. Farberow. Working as a team during the early 1950s, they began to envision a facility that would be dedicated solely to suicide prevention. Anyone in crisis would be welcome there, but the facility would specifically target people who had already attempted suicide. This was based on an exhaustive study conducted by Shneidman and Farberow, during which they found that three-fourths of suicides followed previous suicide threats or attempts. In their paper about the pressing need for this sort of facility, they refer to it as an "emergency psychosocial first aid center—we have compared it with a lifeguard station on a dangerous beach."[20]

Both psychologists were acutely aware that their idea was out of the ordinary and would likely be dismissed by some of their colleagues. They also anticipated that people would question the need for a dedicated suicide prevention center when other resources already existed. "It is legitimate to ask why there should be a separate suicide prevention center," they write. "We know that in most communities there are already available facilities such as hospitals, clinics, social work agencies, professional persons, and more recently, emergency psychiatric centers. Cannot these resources be used optimally to take care of suicidal persons?" Shneidman and Farberow go on to explain that their advocacy of a dedicated center for suicide prevention was consistent with their belief that "the suicidal crisis" had features that were different from other sorts of crises. Specifically, these related to the "dramatically heightened intra- and interpersonal crisis in which life and death frequently hang in the balance."[21]

Schneidman and Farberow achieved their goal when on September 1, 1958, the Los Angeles Suicide Prevention Center opened in an abandoned building on the grounds of the Los Angeles County General Hospital. That same day marked the launch of the facility's twenty-four-hour suicide hotline, which was the first of its kind in the United States. In an article published after the opening of the center, Farberow reflects on the hotline as "the primary means

Within the image:
Hidh Risk
Hidh Risk
Medium Risk
Low Risk
No Risk
At Risk
Codes ↑
Notice
Follow
Ups

of contact with persons needing help." He goes on to describe how the center evolved as word of its existence spread and demand for its services grew: "As the case load zoomed, it forced a basic conceptualization of a suicide prevention center: the center best serves as an emergency, crisis-oriented community agency, focusing on the immediate stressful situation and offering crisis therapy, not long-term rehabilitative care."[22] After seeing what a valuable resource the suicide prevention center had become, Shneidman and Farberow were convinced that every city in the United States should have its own comparable facility. By 1969 the number of centers in the United States had grown to more than one hundred, and within a few years that number had tripled.

A suicide prevention hotline worker takes a call in the 1990s. The first twenty-four-hour suicide hotline began operation in Los Angeles in 1958. In just over a decade, more than one hundred suicide prevention centers were operating around the country, and the numbers continued to grow.

Waning Support

As the nationwide expansion of suicide prevention centers was under way, however, US health officials became concerned about these facilities. They had sprung up so rapidly, and although their creators had the best intentions, the centers often lacked consistent standards for service or training. In 1970 a task force sponsored by the NIMH issued a statement saying that the "establishment of suicide prevention programs was entered into by many who were serious and dedicated but, also, by others who were capricious and ill-advised. The result is a mixture of services which as a whole lack purpose, direction, commitment, and involvement."[23]

Health officials were particularly disturbed by mounting evidence that suicide prevention centers were not doing a good job of preventing suicide. As the number of facilities soared between 1960 and 1970, the overall suicide rate remained essentially the same—and among certain age groups there was even a significant increase in suicides. Youth suicide, for instance, rose from 5.2 percent in 1960 to 8.8 percent in 1970; among twenty- to twenty-four-year-olds, the increase was even more striking, rising from 7.1 to 12.2 percent. Colt writes: "The exaggerated hopes kindled by prevention programs underscored their apparent failure. The centers were discredited as quickly as they had been embraced."[24]

After previously being designated as one of the NIMH's top five priority areas, suicide prevention fell out of favor with the agency and lost support—as well as funding. A new administrator took over as director of the NIMH, and the agency's top priority became child mental health, followed by drug abuse. "Suicide was on its way out," says Colt. "The government, which in ten years had spent more than $10 million on suicide research, decided it was a bad investment."[25]

Revitalized Commitment

The value and importance of a dedicated suicide prevention effort was not forgotten, however. During the 1970s and 1980s health officials still grappled with high suicide rates, which they knew needed to be addressed—but exactly how to do so was a daunting challenge. One major step was the CDC's establishment in 1983 of a violence prevention unit, which was charged with investigating the alarming spike in youth suicide. Other notable happenings during the 1980s included the creation of the American Foundation for Suicide Prevention and the first national suicide awareness memorial, in St. Paul, Minnesota. But it was not until the 1990s that suicide once again became a central issue in the United States, largely due to the efforts of grassroots groups and their citizen-initiated campaign.

These individuals had come together because they shared one important commonality: In some way, each of their lives had been affected by suicide. They included family members of people who had committed suicide, suicide attempt survivors, and community activists who were passionate about helping to prevent suicide. Their collective goal was to establish a private source of support for suicide research and education along with essential suicide prevention efforts that could be sustained into the future. These founding families joined with researchers to create the Suicide Prevention Advocacy Network (SPAN), which in October 1998 convened a national conference on suicide prevention in Reno, Nevada.

The meeting, which came to be known as the Reno Conference, resulted in attendees producing a list of eighty-one recommendations. This led to the US surgeon general's 1999 declaration of suicide as a public health crisis and laid the groundwork for the country's first national strategy for suicide prevention.

> "We believe that suicide is preventable when the right resources and services are in place."[26]
>
> — A joint statement by the US surgeon general and the National Action Alliance for Suicide Prevention.

A Daunting Challenge

In the years since that national strategy was established, other key developments have helped advance suicide prevention in the United States. One, which would certainly have merited the approval of the late suicide prevention pioneers Warren and Shneidman, was the establishment of the National Suicide Prevention Lifeline. This toll-free hotline serves as a central switchboard that seamlessly connects callers to a crisis center as close as possible to their geographic area, choosing from more than 150 of these centers in forty-nine states. Health officials say that these and other strategies can help address America's suicide problem, as a September 2012 report by the US surgeon general and the National Action Alliance for Suicide Prevention states: "We believe that suicide is preventable when the right resources and services are in place. We also recognize that there is a lot of work to do to ensure that those who are most in need receive the services and support they require."[26]

It remains true today that much work in this area is still needed. Despite all that is being done to address the suicide problem in the United States, at least thirty-six thousand people kill themselves each year, and a half million attempt to do so. With such alarming statistics, it is not unusual for people to wonder: What are we doing wrong? What are we missing? What needs to change to solve this problem? Nor is it unusual when those questions cannot be answered with any level of certainty.

Facts

- The first National Survivors of Suicide Day was held in November 1999, and it continues to take place every year on the Saturday before Thanksgiving.

- According to the American Foundation for Suicide Prevention, suicide rates dropped during the twenty-year period from 1990 to 2010 and then rose again to nearly the same rate as 1990.

- Older Americans compose about 13 percent of the US population but account for 18 percent of all suicide deaths.

- According to Mental Health America, those who talk about suicide, threaten suicide, or call suicide crisis centers are thirty times more likely to kill themselves than people who have not done these things.

- According to records kept since 1929, when Nevada began registering vital statistics with the federal government, the state's suicide rate has been two to three times higher than the national rate.

CHAPTER TWO

Should More Resources Be Devoted to Mental Health?

When Kevin Hines was a teenager he began to suffer from severe emotional pain. He had been diagnosed with bipolar disorder and was undergoing treatment, but his medications were not working very well. Like many others with the illness, Hines sometimes became psychotic, meaning he lost touch with reality. So when voices in his head began telling him what to do, he believed that he had to obey—even when the voices said he needed to die. This is what happened in September 2000 when Hines was nineteen years old. One voice in particular, which he describes as "chilling and dangerously demonic," drowned out the rest and began shouting at him. "The voice was like the one I heard as a boy but never told anyone about its existence," he says. "The voice that told me to jump from the Golden Gate Bridge."[27]

Clinging to Life

Hines had lived in San Francisco his whole life, so he was quite familiar with the vivid red-orange suspension bridge that towered over the bay. But on the morning of September 25, 2000, his reason for being there was different from any previous occasion. This time he had gone there with the intention of taking his own life. "I believed I had to," he says. "Compelled by my bipolar disorder, my brain illness, I was to complete this terrible act."[28] Hines rode a bus to the bridge, and on the way—as the voices got louder and more insistent—he sat in the back and cried. He says they were "determined, purposeful, and screaming at me, *You are a horrible person, die now, you must die!* Such self-hatred, such inner turmoil was unbearable."[29]

When Hines's bus arrived at the bridge parking lot, he was suddenly struck by the magnitude of what he was about to do. He reluctantly stepped onto the bridge and began pacing back and forth on the sidewalk, crying and wanting so badly for someone to notice how troubled he was. For more than thirty minutes no one paid any attention; then he noticed a woman walking toward him with a smile on her face. Hines was suddenly hopeful, thinking that the woman was reaching out to him—but when she handed him her camera and asked if he would take her picture, his hope turned to crushing despair. "Nobody cares," he thought, after snapping several pictures and watching her walk away. "Absolutely nobody cares."[30] Then he climbed over the low guardrail and leaped off—and instantly knew he had made a dreadful mistake.

Hurtling through the air at 75 miles per hour (121 kph), Hines was suddenly desperate to save himself. "I somehow possessed the mind-set that *all I wanted to do was live,*" he says. His instincts kicked in, and seconds before he slammed into the wall of water, he threw his head back and twisted his body so he would hit feet first in a sitting position rather than headfirst. The impact, which he says was "like hitting a brick wall at seventy-five miles an hour," broke his back and shattered two lower vertebrae, causing such excruciating pain that he describes it as "unimaginable"[31]—but he did not die. Miraculously, Hines was rescued by the Coast Guard from the choppy waters of San Francisco Bay.

Today Hines is an author and lecturer who travels throughout the United States talking to audiences about his experience and

"For those of you struggling with your mental health, and behavioral health, you have to fight for your life, your existence, for hope."[32]

— Kevin Hines, one of the very few people who survived a jump off the Golden Gate Bridge.

what he learned from it. He is committed to increasing awareness of mental illness, speaking out against the discrimination that is often associated with it, and helping people understand that suicide is never the answer, no matter how unbearable their pain may be. He also makes it clear that mental illness is treatable, and people's lives can change for the better if treatment is available to them. "We need to create more access to care and social inclusion for the mentally ill in our communities and businesses," says Hines. "For those of you struggling with your mental health, and behavioral health, you have to fight for your life, your existence, for hope."[32]

Crucial Accessibility

According to data from the NIMH, Hines is one of nearly 60 million Americans who suffer from some form of mental illness. One of the most common is major depressive disorder (often called

Hundreds of people have jumped to their deaths from San Francisco's famed Golden Gate Bridge. A sign posted above a crisis counseling call box at the bridge urges people contemplating suicide to get help.

CRISIS COUNSELING

THERE IS HOPE
MAKE THE CALL

THE CONSEQUENCES OF JUMPING FROM THIS BRIDGE ARE FATAL AND TRAGIC.

depression), which affects nearly 15 million people. Anxiety disorders, which include post-traumatic stress disorder (PTSD), panic disorder, phobias, and obsessive-compulsive disorder (OCD) are also among the most common mental illnesses, affecting some 40 million Americans. Less prevalent are severe, incapacitating mental illnesses such as bipolar disorder and schizophrenia, which together affect about 8 million Americans.

Mental health experts widely acknowledge the close association between mental illness and suicide. According to the American Foundation for Suicide Prevention, at least 90 percent of all people who have committed suicide were suffering from some form of mental illness—most commonly depression—at the time of their deaths. The group adds: "Among people who are depressed, intense emotional states such as desperation, hopelessness, anxiety, or rage increase the risk of suicide. People who are impulsive, or who use alcohol and drugs, are also at higher risk."[33] Because of the link between mental illness and suicidal behavior, it is imperative for those who are affected by mental illness to have access to resources that can help them.

Calling for Help

One of the most accessible resources for people who are struggling with any sort of emotional distress and/or suicidal thoughts is the National Suicide Prevention Lifeline. Funded by the Substance Abuse and Mental Health Services Administration (SAMHSA), the lifeline is operational twenty-four hours a day, seven days a week, and provides free, confidential support to all who seek it. Although the lifeline's headquarters is in New York City, it is actually a network of more than 160 independently operating call centers in all fifty US states. Someone calling the toll-free number is rerouted to the crisis center that is closest to his or her geographic location. Operators are trained in risk assessment skills, so they can consistently and quickly determine the seriousness of a situation during the conversation. Depending on the need, the caller may be referred to a mental health treatment facility or other resources.

Although it is difficult for experts to accurately gauge the effectiveness of the lifeline, research suggests that the service can

The British Coal-Gas Story

Mental illness, especially depression, has long been known as a major contributor to suicide. Although this is widely accepted, it has also been challenged because of the role impulsivity plays: Someone makes a split-second decision to die without planning it beforehand. To show the validity of this theory, proponents often refer to what is known as the British coal-gas story. For decades, gas that was derived from coal (known as coal-gas) was Britain's primary fuel. It was both plentiful and cheap, but because coal-gas released extremely high levels of carbon monoxide it was also deadly—and its use led to asphyxiation being the preferred method of suicide in Britain. People simply turned on the gas, stuck their heads in an oven, breathed in the poisonous fumes, and died within minutes.

After natural gas was discovered beneath the North Sea, the British government phased out the use of coal-gas. Suicides by asphyxiation plummeted, and by 1978 the country's overall suicide rate had dropped by nearly one-third. Journalist Scott Anderson writes in a July 2008 *New York Times* article: "In a moment of deep despair or rage or sadness, they turned to what was easy and quick and deadly—'the execution chamber in everyone's kitchen,' as one psychologist described it—and that instrument allowed little time for second thoughts. Remove it, and the process slowed down; it allowed time for the dark passion to pass."

Scott Anderson, "The Urge to End It All," *New York Times*, July 6, 2008. www.nytimes.com.

help deter someone from committing suicide. One researcher who has explored this is Madelyn Gould, a child and adolescent psychologist from Columbia University. Gould and her colleagues analyzed follow-up interviews with people in crisis who had called the lifeline, and 12 percent of suicidal callers said that being able to talk to and make a personal connection with someone who cared prevented them from harming or killing themselves. Another finding was that nearly half of respondents followed through with a counselor's referral to either seek emergency services or contact a mental health provider, and about 80 percent said that in some way the lifeline played a role in keeping them alive.

According to John Draper, a psychologist who directs the national lifeline program, these findings are consistent with what he and his staff hear from people who have used the service. "I don't know if we'll ever have solid evidence for what saves lives other than people saying they saved my life," says Draper. "It may be that the suicide rate could be higher if crisis lines weren't in effect. I don't know. All I can say is that what we're hearing from callers is that this is having a real life-saving impact."[34]

Treatment Options

The lifeline can be ideal for people who need immediate help with a crisis situation or those who are suffering from any sort of emotional trauma. Those who battle mental illness on a daily basis, however, need different kinds of resources. Throughout the United States, many types of mental health resources are available to serve people who need them, although the particular offering can vary widely from state to state and from community to community. Typically, patients are referred for mental health consultation and treatment by a family physician, emergency room physician, caseworker, or someone from law enforcement if the patient has gotten into legal trouble.

One example of a regional network of resources is the Mental Health Association of Central Oklahoma, which is headquartered in Oklahoma City. It acts as a gateway to the region's wide array of mental health resources and serves an estimated thirty-five thousand people each year. Within the network are numerous counseling facilities staffed by trained and certified therapists (such as psychiatrists, psychologists, and/or social workers) who are qualified to counsel children, adolescents, and adults. Depending on the patient's need, these professionals can provide many different types of therapy on an individual basis, as well as group and family therapy.

For patients who require more intensive treatment, the central Oklahoma network offers several residential facilities. One "in-between" program offered through St. Anthony Hospital in Oklahoma City is called Stages. It is designed for people who may not need the twenty-four-hour monitoring of inpatient treatment but still require a highly structured outpatient environment. Patients take part in individualized treatment planning, individual and group therapy, and a variety of enrichment activities, among other services. Transportation to the facility can be provided for those who lack it.

Although these particular resources are located in central Oklahoma, they are indicative of the types of mental health services that may also be found in other communities throughout the United States. Such programs and facilities have proved to help people with mental illness overcome their obstacles and live happier, healthier lives.

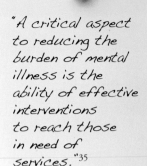

"A critical aspect to reducing the burden of mental illness is the ability of effective interventions to reach those in need of services."[35]

— Alan E. Kazdin and Sarah M. Rabbitt, psychologists from Yale University.

Roadblocks

The unfortunate reality, however, is that these resources are not accessible to the majority of people who need them. This has been shown in a number of studies, such as one conducted by Yale University psychologists Alan E. Kazdin and Sarah M. Rabbitt. The study found that up to 70 percent of people in the United States who suffer from mental illness have no access to treatment. In their 2013 report on the study, Kazdin and Rabbitt write: "A critical aspect to reducing the burden of mental illness is the ability of effective interventions to reach those in need of services."[35]

There are a number of reasons why so many people who suffer from mental disorders are not treated. One of the main reasons people give is the stigma associated with these illnesses, which discourages many who need help from reaching out for it. This was one of the revelations of a SAMHSA study that was published in January 2013. Of nearly 5 million people who did not receive needed treatment for mental illness, 30 percent said it was because they were afraid of the consequences, including negative effects on their jobs or being viewed negatively by neighbors or the community. Harvard Medical School psychiatrist Joseph Shrand shares his thoughts about this stigmatization: "The real barriers to people not getting help has to do with the entire stigma of mental illness—treating people as if they have a deviation and must pull themselves up by the bootstraps."[36]

The fear of being stigmatized is also a deterrent to young people who need treatment for mental illness. In fact, numerous barriers keep children and adolescents from having access to the mental health resources they need. According to a January 2013 publication by the research group Child Trends, between 60 and 90 percent of youth with mental disorders fail to receive treatment. The authors write: "Multiple challenges exist in trying to connect adolescents with mental health disorders to the services and treatments that can help them attain a better quality of life."[37] Some other hurdles faced by youth who need mental health services include missed opportunities by parents, school officials, and medical providers to identify mental health disorders; lack of health insurance or restrictions by insurers on coverage for certain services, such as mental health treatment; and shortages of providers who specialize in adolescent mental health.

"The real barriers to people not getting help has to do with the entire stigma of mental illness— treating people as if they have a deviation and must pull themselves up by the bootstraps."[36]

— Joseph Shrand, a psychiatrist with Harvard Medical School.

Budget Tightening by Feds

Of all the challenges that impede people's ability to tap into mental health services, none is more daunting than being unable to afford those services. In recent years the recession has necessitated drastic spending cuts by the federal government, which in turn has led to cuts in funding for public mental health programs. As a result, only people who have superior health insurance policies and/or enough money to pay for whatever services they need are able to take advantage of the best treatment. A July 2011 SAM-HSA paper explains: "For many individuals with mental health problems, their willingness to seek and their success in receiving treatment often depend on their ability to pay, either from their

own resources or through private or public insurance coverage. Appropriate treatment may be inaccessible because individuals lack any insurance coverage, or the insurance coverage they have for mental health and substance abuse conditions is inadequate."[38]

Even though spending cuts may be necessary, many experts argue that taking money away from mental health programs is shortsighted thinking. They warn that by making it difficult, or even impossible, for most mentally ill people to access treatment, society will end up paying a hefty price in the long run. The National Alliance on Mental Illness (NAMI) writes: "Effective mental

A high school student talks with a psychologist. Counseling services are available to youth and adults in communities all across the nation.

health services, like other types of health services, require resources and a high-quality system of care, and therefore cannot be achieved without adequate funding. Analyses of public funding have shown that the failure to fund mental health services adequately results in significantly greater funding being required in other systems, such as child welfare, jails and prisons, and emergency rooms, to address the consequences of untreated mental illness."[39]

In the United States the primary funding agency for the federal government is the National Institutes of Health (NIH). In recent years the agency has been sharply criticized by mental health advocates and suicide prevention agencies for its research priorities, which allocate little of the agency's overall budget to suicide. Comparisons are often drawn between the small amount earmarked for suicide-related programs and the funding for diseases. In an August 2010 *Forbes* article journalists Robert Langreth and Rebecca Ruiz state that the NIH is "spending a paltry $40 million in 2010 studying suicide, versus $3.1 billion for research on AIDS, which kills half the number of Americans."[40] For the year 2014 the NIH did increase funding for suicide and suicide prevention to $66 million. Still, this is much less than allocations for diseases that cause far fewer deaths per year than does suicide. The 2014 allocation for prostate cancer, for instance, was $259 million in 2014, and for tuberculosis it was $219 million.

People Are Hurting

When federal funding for mental health is slashed, less money is allocated to the states, so they, too, must make tough decisions about which programs to fund—and mental health programs bear the brunt of the cuts. According to NAMI, between 2009 and 2011 states cut more than $4 billion in mental health spending, which has wreaked havoc on programs that serve millions of people suffering from mental illness. The state that has fared worse than any other is South Carolina. From 2009 to 2011 the mental health budget was cut from $187.3 million to $113.7 million—nearly a 40 percent drop in funding. According to Bill Lindsey, the executive director of NAMI's South Carolina chapter, his department "is approaching crisis mode with funding at

A Vision Never Realized

On October 31, 1963, when President John F. Kennedy signed the Community Mental Health Act into law, his intent was to benefit severely mentally ill Americans. The legislation called for them to be treated in their own communities rather than housed in institutions as they traditionally had been. This would happen through the elimination of psychiatric beds in public hospitals and the subsequent construction of fifteen hundred community mental health centers. The planned result would be significant cost reductions, balanced by the assurance that people who needed mental health care would receive it in a way that was more humane and conducive to their recovery.

Kennedy was assassinated less than one month later, so he never saw how the legislation failed to achieve what he had envisioned. Mental health care funding was indeed reduced over the following years, but this did not lead to improved care for the mentally ill. When hospitals eliminated psychiatric beds, patients had nowhere to go because most of the community mental health centers were never built. Thus, tens of thousands of mentally ill individuals ended up homeless or in prison—or dead from taking their own lives. Several studies have examined the effects of deinstitutionalization and showed a link to higher suicide rates. In one 2009 study researchers Jangho Yoon and Tim A. Bruckner calculated that a decrease of one psychiatric bed per one hundred thousand people (approximately 1,818 beds nationwide) would result in forty-five additional suicides per year.

1987 levels," as he explains: "These cuts mean that clinics, crisis centers and hospitals get closed. Admissions are frozen. . . . Even where services remain, staff is cut, wait times for appointments are stretched."[41]

Maryland is another state with severe funding problems. The perception of many who work in the mental health field is that these problems are due to misguided priorities on the part of state government officials. In 2013 Maryland's governor announced that he was revoking $7.2 million that had already been earmarked for state psychiatric services. As a result, the state now provides less money for mental health programs than for other types of medical care, which has hurt the state's mentally ill population. Steve Daviss, who is chairman of psychiatry at the Baltimore-Washington Medical Center, says that people are waiting longer and longer before seeking treatment. "They go until they just can't function anymore," says Daviss, "or until they are forced to get help."[42]

A Dismal Situation

There is no doubt that the mental health system in the United States is plagued by serious problems. Although there are many options for treatment, these resources are not available to most people who need them. Mental health specialists and advocacy organizations caution that when the needs of the mentally ill are not being met, it can lead to tragic results. Daviss has personally witnessed this, as he explains: "Many of my patients are people at the end of their rope, and they are ready to kill themselves. They say, 'I can't get the help I need.'"[43]

Facts

- Suicide Awareness Voices of Education (SAVE) says that 15 percent of people who are clinically depressed die by suicide.

- Mental Health America says that completed suicides are most likely to be men over forty-five years old who are depressed or alcoholic.

- NIMH director Thomas Insel says the rate of suicide among men with bipolar disorder is about 7 percent, which rises to 17 percent when combined with substance abuse.

- According to the NIMH, a type of psychotherapy called cognitive therapy has been shown to reduce the rate of repeated suicide attempts by 50 percent during a year of follow-up.

- The American Academy of Child & Adolescent Psychiatry says many of the signs and symptoms of suicidal feelings are similar to those of depression.

- Mental Health America reports that the risk of death by suicide is more than one hundred times greater than average in the first year after an attempted suicide.

CHAPTER THREE

How Effective Are Youth Suicide Prevention Efforts?

The first time Gretchen Cheverton thought about suicide she was only eight years old, and it was her birthday. "I stood in front of a homemade cake, surrounded by my loving family, and made my wish as I blew out the candles," she says. "I wished to die."[44] Cheverton says that nothing about her life caused the despair she was feeling as a young child. She always knew her parents loved her. She had never been abused or neglected. She had been encouraged to explore and use her creativity while having the security of firm boundaries. There was no apparent reason for such unbearable sadness, yet she was consumed by it.

Six years after that birthday, when Cheverton had just turned fourteen, the emotional pain finally became overwhelming. Feeling that she could stand it no more she took an overdose of pills. Fortunately she was discovered in time and rushed to the hospital, where emergency medical staff saved her life. She says that being stopped from killing herself was "simply a matter of luck and poor planning" on her part. "I wasn't trying to get attention or trying to manipulate the people around me, as I was later accused," she says. "I was simply trying to end the pain and hopelessness that had consumed my life."[45] What Cheverton did not know at the time was that her emotional pain was a symptom of bipolar disorder.

Out of the Shadows

Years passed before Cheverton was diagnosed and treated for her illness, and today she is doing well. She has become an outspoken advocate for widespread education and awareness programs, because when she was growing up, suicide was considered taboo, a subject that no one ever talked about. Cheverton cannot help wondering how different things might have been if the topic had been openly discussed. Perhaps she would have learned that other young people were suffering, too, which would have kept her from feeling so isolated. "My health class talked about birth control, nutrition, STDs and drug abuse, but not mental health," she says. "And certainly not suicide. I was so lonely and so ashamed. I was so ill-equipped to help myself. I wanted someone to tell me that I wasn't alone."[46]

Cheverton is glad to see the expansion of suicide prevention efforts that are helping to bring suicide out into the open. She cautions, however, that there is still a long way to go before the problem of youth suicide is even close to being resolved, largely because of how society views mental illness. "There are two things that stand in the way of effective treatment," she says. "Stigma and ignorance. People still don't think of mental illness as a treatable medical condition and they don't know how to deal with it when it happens. So they hide it. And in doing so they fail to treat it. And kids die."[47]

Kids are indeed dying by suicide—thousands each year, in fact. Daniel Taylor, a pediatrician with St. Christopher's Hospital for Children and associate professor at Drexel College of Medicine, writes: "From 1999 to 2010, 22,993 children 5 to 19 years old took their lives, leaving an empty space of agony for family

> "People still don't think of mental illness as a treatable medical condition and they don't know how to deal with it when it happens. So they hide it."[47]

— Gretchen Cheverton, a Colorado woman who first had suicidal thoughts when she was just eight years old.

A group of teens places flowers at the site where three young people jumped to their deaths. Suicide is the third leading cause of death for youth, behind accidental injuries and homicide.

and friends that can never be filled."[48] According to the NIH, suicide is the third leading cause of death for youth, surpassed only by accidental injuries and homicide. CDC data show that each year an estimated forty-six hundred youth take their own lives and thousands more have suicidal thoughts and/or attempt suicide. With such bleak statistics, experts say it is more crucial than ever for the topic of suicide to be brought out of the shadows and discussed openly and honestly.

Tragedy Breeds Action

Open and honest discussions about youth suicide have made an enormous difference in the small California town of Indian Valley—but it took unspeakable tragedy to bring that about. The community, which has a large Native American population, is about 250 miles (402.3 km) northeast of San Francisco and is tucked into the Sierra Nevadas. During a two-year period Indian Valley was rocked by the suicides of six teenage boys. The last one, Nate Cunningham, killed himself during the winter of 2011. In an article about the tragedies, journalist Jane Braxton Little says that this "shook [the] rural community like an earthquake. Home to ranchers, loggers, and retirees, it is a place where almost everyone knows everyone else, often across several generations. The dead boys were sons of Indian Valley. Some were gentle, others pranksters. Some played sports, others dabbled in music. All but one were Maidu Indians."[49]

The people of Indian Valley hoped for some kind of crisis response from social service providers, but they heard nothing. The high school offered one day of grief counseling, and the Maidu education center held a day-long event with healers and dancers, but that was all. "No discussion for parents, no suicide prevention training for teachers, nothing to kick-start the painful process of healing," says Little. "A close-knit community of 3,000 residents, Indian Valley had rallied together after forest fires, floods, and the threatened closure of the area's only high school. The suicides, however, seemed to drive people into isolation."[50] Although most residents remained silent about what had happened, Marsha Ebersole and Susie Wilson were not willing to do that. Ebersole's son Ethan was best friends with Cunningham and terribly distraught over his death, and Wilson had previously lost her husband, brother, and several close friends to suicide. Together, they vowed to get the community talking and find a way to save young people from the senseless, tragic act of suicide.

In January 2012 the two women held a community-wide meeting that drew about eighty-five people. Attendees included parents, educators, students, the county mental health director,

The Antidepressant Controversy

Screening for depression in schools has been praised because it ensures that young people with the illness are diagnosed and treated at an early stage. In many cases, though, treatment involves antidepressant medications, and some mental health specialists question the wisdom of prescribing them for youth. These concerns largely stem from a 2003 study by the Food and Drug Administration (FDA), which found that antidepressants increased suicidality (suicidal thoughts and actions) in youth. As a result, the FDA now mandates that the drugs be labeled with a "black box" warning, which is the most serious type of warning in prescription drug labeling.

In November 2010 eighteen-year-old Brennan McCartney committed suicide after taking an antidepressant called Lexapro. He had gone to the family doctor because of a head cold, and during their visit he mentioned feeling sad over a breakup with his girlfriend. The doctor gave him samples of the antidepressant, and when his parents found out they were shocked. Brennan was known to be fun-loving and good-natured, and he never hesitated to express his feelings. People closest to him did not believe he was depressed, nor did they think he should be taking the drug. So when he killed himself, his parents were convinced that it was because of the Lexapro.

elders of the Maidu tribe, and the county sheriff. "This was an outpouring of heartbreak,"[51] says Wilson. The community gathering spawned the formation of the Indian Valley Youth Summit, a grassroots group that began meeting on a regular basis. It became the county's first and only organization devoted entirely to suicide awareness and prevention.

As positive and hopeful as everyone was about the Youth Summit, participation began to wane not long after it was formed.

Some members who were enthusiastic at the beginning lost interest. Assistance that was promised by the county mental health department and Native American organizations never materialized. Despite these setbacks, however, the two founders were driven by passion for their cause and were not about to be defeated. "Somebody has to do this," says Wilson. "We will not allow our youth to be dismissed."[52]

Young Lives Saved

As the months passed, however, the Indian Valley Youth Summit began to grow in strength. Ebersole and Wilson organized the county's first suicide prevention training for teens and also matched young people with adult mentors to serve as positive role models. A local rancher came up with the idea of "no-suicide contracts" for youth and designed a wallet card listing the name and phone number of a "survival buddy." Teenagers who signed the contracts pledged not to harm themselves, and they promised to call their buddies if they had suicidal thoughts.

Soon other grassroots groups began springing up throughout the community, and more people became involved. Support also came from the county mental health department, which provided funding for expansion of the mentor program and a new community center for teens. Another strong supporter was the superintendent of schools. She helped organize assemblies on bullying and suicide at local high schools and directed teachers to develop suicide-prevention curricula. "The doors have flown open in the last few months," says Wilson. "We have grown from a mentality that wouldn't let us talk about suicide to a program about suicide that's countywide."[53]

As the problem of youth suicide went from being a taboo subject to one that was regularly discussed, its effect on the Indian Valley community was profound. Some high school students chose to focus on suicide for class assignments. Terra Adcock, for example, hosted an all-school assembly about the signs of depression. Ryllie Cantrell studied the effect of weather on suicide rates, and her sister created and

"We have grown from a mentality that wouldn't let us talk about suicide to a program about suicide that's countywide."[53]

— Susie Wilson, one of two residents of Indian Valley, California, who developed the community's first youth suicide prevention program.

implemented a presentation on the psychological impact of bullying. Other students have tackled the topic as well. By far the most important measure of the Indian Valley suicide prevention effort's success is young lives saved: Since January 2012, when the endeavor first began, not a single young person has been lost to suicide. "The little youth group that critics so belittled is saving lives,"[54] says Wilson.

Kids Saving Kids

Indian Valley's prevention effort has succeeded for a number of reasons, one of which is the interest and involvement of young people. Similar endeavors are happening throughout the country, with teens becoming more aware of how they can help stop youth suicide. Sometimes this involves nothing more than tuning in to warning signals that young people give off without even realizing it. Although teens who take their own lives may do so without giving any indication ahead of time, this is rare. Far more common is for youth to drop hints or give some kind of sign that they are in distress, perhaps even threatening to harm themselves. Unfortunately, though, studies have shown that when teens do come out and make suicide threats, they are often not taken seriously—and that can be deadly. Parents, educators, and friends who hear such a threat must err on the side of caution and assume that the teen is 100 percent serious, even if he or she denies it.

In May 2013 the life of a sixteen-year-old girl from Union Township, New Jersey, was saved by another teenage girl from the opposite side of the country. For about a year eighteen-year-old Jackie Rosas, who lives in Cathedral City, California, had been following the blog of the New Jersey girl on the Tumblr site. Rosas had seen people bullying her anonymously on the site, and on the afternoon of May 6 the girl posted a blog entry about her intent to commit suicide. "She blogged, saying that she was going to end her life," says Rosas. "When she posted that, my instinct was that she was serious. She wrote something like, 'I'm going to kill myself. There is no other option.'"[55]

The girl's post shocked and frightened Rosas, and she was desperate to do something. She called a local suicide hotline, but no one there could help since she did not know the girl's last name or where she lived. The operator advised her to call the police, which she did. While speaking with officer Kelly Nava, Rosas gave her the web address for the blog on Tumblr and the girl's first name. Nava went to work, searching and networking with others in law enforcement. She learned that the girl had a Twitter account where her last name appeared, and by digging through her blog posts and tweets she found out where the girl lived. The police department in Union Township was notified and sent officers to the girl's address. At 1:30 in the morning, eight hours after Rosas reported the suicide threat, Nava heard back from them. The girl had been rushed to the hospital because she had taken a large quantity of pills, but she was expected to recover. Rosas, who was commended by the police for her quick thinking, was thrilled to know that the girl would be okay. "I kind of cried," she says. "I was happy to know that I saved someone's life. It happened at random and it's an amazing feeling knowing you are able to help someone from thousands of miles away."[56]

> "It's an amazing feeling knowing you are able to help someone from thousands of miles away."[56]
>
> — Jackie Rosas, a young woman from Cathedral City, California, who saved the life of a teenage girl from New Jersey who blogged about her plan to commit suicide.

Screening Saves Lives

Before the New Jersey teen's suicide threat Rosas had noticed that she often posted about her struggles with depression. That was not surprising, since the illness has a very close association with suicidal thoughts and behavior. Studies have shown that it is much more common among teens than many people realize and is a leading contributor to youth suicide. According to the organization Mental Health America (MHA), 90 percent of young people who die by suicide suffer from a treatable mental illness, most often depression, and 65 percent experience symptoms for a full year prior to their death. Leading child and adolescent psychiatrist Harold Koplewicz writes: "We often hear that suicide is the third leading cause of death—after accidents and homicide—among teens and young adults between 15 and 24 years of age. What we don't often hear is that over 90 percent of all young people who commit suicide are suffering from severe mental illness.

Depression is the leading condition in the suicides of adolescent boys and girls."[57]

In an effort to identify depression at an early stage and hopefully save lives, mental health experts and advocacy groups have called for significantly increased depression screenings among teenagers. Such screenings are invaluable for catching depression at an early stage, even before symptoms are apparent. Because of that, the depression screenings are recommended by the US Preventive Services Task Force, which is an independent panel of nongovernmental experts. In March 2009 the group announced its recommendation that all adolescents aged twelve to eighteen be screened for depression as long as systems are in place to ensure accurate diagnosis, treatment, and follow-up. A number of these programs have been developed, such as one offered by the MHA called Youth Screen. This prevention and intervention program is designed to reduce new incidences of major depression, anxiety disorders, and substance abuse among children and adolescents. Since 2007 the Youth Screen program has been in place in Chicago-area schools, financed by local organizations and MHA Illinois.

The first phase of the process is youth education, during which a program director visits classrooms and speaks to students about mental health and mental illness. The director returns to the classroom the following day and gives students the opportunity to fill out a confidential, personal questionnaire that has fourteen questions. How students answer the questions helps Youth Screen staff identify which of them are at risk for developing major depression, an anxiety disorder, and/or a substance abuse disorder. Once these students have been identified, their parents are notified and given information about appropriate academic and social services in the school and the community. Program staff members follow up and support parents throughout the process of scheduling and transporting the student to the crucial first appointment. If a student is deemed to be at risk for suicide, parents are immediately informed, as are school officials.

Since Youth Screen was implemented in 2007 more than 3,000 students in Chicago-area schools have been screened. Of those,

Depression is closely linked to suicidal thoughts and actions. It is a leading contributor to youth suicide.

600 were found to be at risk for depression, and nearly 140 were identified as having current suicidal thoughts or previous suicide attempts. Teachers and administrators have praised the program. One high school principal states: "Screening has made such a difference in the social/emotional health of our students. We were made aware of issues that might have otherwise gone unknown and I truly believe that our students' lives are better for the resources that were shared thanks to the work of Youth Screen."[58]

Mental Health Intervention

Screening programs are extremely valuable because they can identify youth who are at high risk for suicide before a suicide attempt has been made. Also valuable are mental health interventions that

Suicidal Kids Not Getting Treatment

Mental health specialists emphasize that suicidal youth could benefit greatly from treatment, but a study published in 2011 found that the majority are not receiving the care they need. Conducted by a team of researchers from Seattle Children's Research Institute, the study focused on the use of health care services among 198 adolescents aged thirteen to seventeen. Half of the teens had experienced suicidal thinking and the other half had not.

At the conclusion of the study the team found that the usage of mental health services was low. Although 86 percent of the youth with suicidal thoughts had seen a health care provider, only 13 percent had been treated by a mental health specialist. This was true even though the suicidal teens were found to have a high incidence of depression and/or anxiety. Says lead researcher Carolyn A. McCarty: "These findings underscore the need for clinicians to be aware of the potential for suicide in adolescence. Primary care physicians and healthcare providers should be specifically assessing suicidal ideation in the context of depression screening for teenagers. Effective screening tools are available, as are effective treatments for depression."

Quoted in Seattle Children's Research Institute, "Study Finds over 70 Percent of Suicidal Teens Don't Get the Mental Health Services They Need," September 13, 2011. www.seattlechildrens.org.

can help young people who have attempted suicide receive the follow-up care they need. This was the focus of a 2011 study conducted by a team of researchers from the University of California, Los Angeles. The team found that a family-based intervention that was conducted while youths were still being treated in emergency departments led to dramatic improvements in linking them to outpatient treatment following their discharge.

Joan Asarnow, a UCLA professor of psychiatry and lead researcher for the study, explains why this was an important finding: "Youths who are treated for suicidal behavior in emergency departments are at very high risk for future attempts." Asarnow goes on to say that a large proportion of young people who are seen in emergency departments for suicide do not go on to receive outpatient treatment after discharge. "So," she says, "a national objective is to increase the rates of mental health follow-up treatment for suicidal patients coming out of emergency departments."[59]

In conducting the study, Asarnow's team studied 181 suicidal youths (average age, fifteen) at two emergency departments in Los Angeles County. For 53 percent of the youth, the emergency department visit was due to a suicide attempt, while the remainder were seen because they had suicidal thoughts. The young people were randomly assigned to either the standard emergency department treatment or an enhanced mental health intervention. The latter involved a family-based crisis-therapy session designed to increase motivation for outpatient follow-up treatment as well as improve the youths' safety, and it was supplemented by telephone support. The team discovered that the enhanced mental health intervention was associated with higher rates of follow-up treatment. Says Asarnow: "The results underscore the urgent need for improved community outpatient treatment for suicidal youths."[60]

Saving Kids from Themselves

Any time a young person dies it is tragic, no matter what caused the death. But for a teen to become so despondent, so consumed with pain and hopelessness that dying seems like the only way to escape, is especially heartbreaking. With growing awareness of youth suicide, combined with expanding efforts to prevent it, the situation is much improved compared with the past. Still, however, thousands of youth are taking their own lives each year, which means that the problem is a long way from being solved.

Facts

- According to the American Academy of Child & Adolescent Psychiatry, suicide is the sixth leading cause of death for children aged five to fourteen.

- Suicide Awareness Voices of Education (SAVE) reports that between 1952 and 1995, suicide among young adults nearly tripled.

- Of the reported suicides in the ten- to twenty-four-year-old age group, 81 percent were males and 19 percent were females.

- According to the NGA Center for Best Practices, US states spend nearly $1 billion annually on medical costs associated with completed suicides and suicide attempts by youth under twenty years of age.

- According to the CDC, the top three methods used by youths who commit suicide are firearms (45 percent), suffocation (40 percent), and poisoning (8 percent).

- The Ohio Department of Mental Health reports that over 20 percent of high school students have seriously considered suicide, 14 percent have made a plan, and 8 percent have attempted suicide.

CHAPTER FOUR

Should Suicide Prevention Be a Higher Priority for the Military?

F rom the time Danny Weiss was fifteen years old, he knew exactly what he wanted to do for a living: serve his country by wearing the uniform of the United States Army. This goal began to take shape in his mind after the September 11, 2001, terrorist attacks on the United States, which affected him deeply. "He was clearly moved by 9/11," says his mother, Julianne. "He hated the smallness and superficiality of high school compared to what was going on in the world. He had a more mature view of the world than some kids his age."[61] In 2004 Weiss graduated from high school a semester early and, as he had planned, enlisted in the army.

Weiss was first deployed to Afghanistan in 2005, and he served two more tours of duty after that. Between deployments he attended college and earned a bachelor's degree and then completed officer candidate school, where he achieved the rank of first lieutenant. By the time he was twenty-five Weiss had earned almost every possible honor, including the National Defense Service Medal, Army Commendation Medal, Army Service Ribbon, the NATO Medal, and Airborne Wings. His performance evaluations were exemplary, with his most recent one stating, "Stellar, shining, ready to be promoted to captain immediately."[62] All service members who reported to Weiss loved and respected him. He seemed happy, and it appeared to others that his life was going exceptionally well. But on the evening of March 4, 2012, in Fort Lewis, Washington, Weiss put a gun to his head and shot himself to death.

A Family Gives Back

The Tragedy Assistance Program for Survivors (TAPS) offers support to families of military men and women who have committed suicide. Pictured is a young girl's letter to her father. During a TAPS event, the letter was attached to a red balloon and then released.

Like others who are left behind in the wake of a suicide, Weiss's devastated family could only wonder why. Had he developed post-traumatic stress disorder (PTSD) from exposure to the horrors of war? Was he suffering from severe emotional pain that no one knew about? His parents and brother felt totally lost, as his father Andy explains: "Early in our grief, our physical and emotional toll was such that we were in a very dense fog and unable to see things clearly."[63] Knowing that they needed help badly, the family turned to two groups: Survivors of Suicide and a military support group, Tragedy Assistance Program for Survivors (TAPS).

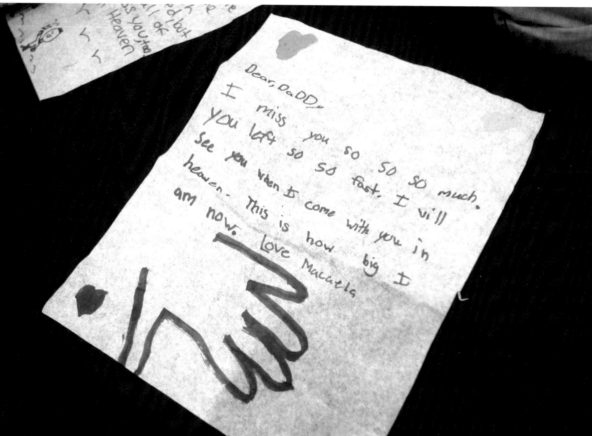

These two organizations were a godsend for the Weiss family in helping them cope with their grief and get back to living again. They, in turn, decided to reach out to other families who were grieving by becoming TAPS volunteers. Today, they work with service members and veterans who may be at risk for suicide. Because Danny Weiss exhibited no visible signs of being suicidal, his parents are well aware that military people can be suffering from what have been called invisible wounds. "Their wounds are not invisible," says Andy Weiss. "You just have to look harder."[64]

A Growing Crisis

A disturbing fact, according to the Department of Veterans Affairs, is that on the day Danny Weiss took his own life, twenty-one other military service members did the same. Also alarming is a statistic that was revealed by military officials in December 2012: That year, for the first time in history, more military personnel died by suicide than were killed in combat. Retired US Army generals Dennis J. Reimer and Peter W. Chiarelli write: "Suicides have become an epidemic. This year, more soldiers, seamen, airmen and Marines died by their own hands than died in battle. Suicide was the No. 1 cause of death for U.S. troops."[65]

NIMH director Thomas Insel is concerned about the fact that military suicides have surpassed combat deaths. "That's not just because combat deaths have been coming down, which they have," says Insel, "but because suicides have become high and have stayed high. Examining suicide in the military is probably the single biggest project at NIMH these days."[66] Insel adds that identifying the root cause of the suicide problem is no easy task. Theories abound, including multiple deployments, personal losses while deployed (such as divorce or death of a loved one), post-combat trauma, and a number of other factors. He explains:

"This year, more soldiers, seamen, airmen and Marines died by their own hands than died in battle."[65]

— Dennis J. Reimer and Peter W. Chiarelli, retired US Army generals.

It's complicated, and none of those theories have panned out so far. It turns out that there is not a single explanation for the increasing rate. . . . Most people think they know what's driving the suicide rate in the Army but all the data we have so far says this really needs to be examined very carefully, that many of our assumptions have been wrong. As we've looked at the first 500 suicides from the past decade, there's not a single or even two or three factors—it's many factors.[67]

Deployment Theory Debunked

Multiple deployments are often blamed for military service members taking their own lives, but Insel says that really cannot explain such a high number of suicides. "In fact," he says, "we've been surprised to find out how many of the suicides occur before there are any deployments."[68] Evaluating the validity of the multiple deployments theory was the focus of a 2013 study that was conducted by Cynthia A. LeardMann of the Naval Health Research Center and her colleagues. Many people were astonished to hear that multiple deployments were not implicated in the suicides of military personnel.

LeardMann's team examined the prevalence of suicide among a large population of current and former military personnel from all service branches. The factors found to be closely associated with suicide included depression, bipolar disorder, heavy or binge drinking, and other alcohol-related problems. None of the factors related to deployment, including the number of deployments, cumulative days deployed, or combat experience, were found to be linked to suicide. "Many people might be surprised by these results," says LeardMann, "but my colleagues and I really weren't surprised based on what we know about the people who have committed suicide. Most suicides happen among troops who have not seen combat."[69]

"Most suicides happen among troops who have not seen combat."[69]

— Cynthia A. LeardMann, a researcher with the Naval Health Research Center in San Diego, California.

The Root of the Problem

Not so surprising was the study's finding about the connection between suicide and depression, bipolar disorder, and alcohol-related problems. Mental illnesses and substance abuse have long been associated with suicidal thinking and behavior, and the study sup-

Regrettable Remarks

As the number of military suicides has continued to soar, officials in all branches of service have made a commitment to help solve the problem. One area of focus is stigma, which is a pervasive problem in the military. Service members struggling with emotional issues often avoid asking for help out of fear that they will be considered weak and unfit to serve. Military leaders have spoken out, saying that stigma must be eliminated—which is why a January 2012 blog post from Major General Dana Pittard was so disturbing. In his post, Pittard said he had come to the conclusion "that suicide is an absolutely selfish act. Soldiers who commit suicide leave their families, their buddies and their units to literally clean up their mess." Pittard went on to say that he was "personally fed up with Soldiers who are choosing to take their own lives. . . . Be an adult, act like an adult, and deal with your real-life problems like the rest of us."

Pittard's post led to a backlash of criticism. Many of his acquaintances were surprised, saying that he is known for being sensitive to service members' needs, and his remarks were out of character. Pittard later wrote a retraction in which he apologized and offered words of encouragement: "We can all help by wrapping our arms around our fellow soldiers and showing them a future that is positive and supportive. This takes both leadership and compassion."

Quoted in Larry Shaughnessy, "General's Remarks About Suicide 'Upsetting,'" CNN *Security Clearance* (blog), May 25, 2012. http://security.blogs.cnn.com.

ports that. In the August 2013 published report the authors write: "The most important finding was that mental health problems, including [bipolar] disorder, depression, and alcohol-related problems, were significantly associated with an increase in the risk of suicide."[70] A curious finding was that PTSD, which is one of the most severe, debilitating mental illnesses for military personnel, was not shown to be a leading factor in suicide. Only 10 percent of the service members studied had experienced PTSD symptoms compared with 66 percent with drinking problems.

Depression, however, was closely linked to suicide, which is the case not only among military personnel but the population in general. Depression can be a dangerous mental illness because people who have symptoms may not realize what is wrong and avoid seeking help. Major General Mark Graham, who retired from the US Army after more than thirty years of service, is well aware of the dangers of depression because his son Kevin suffered from it—and took his own life when he was twenty-one years old.

Kevin was a Reserve Officers' Training Corps cadet at the University of Kentucky whose dream was to become a military doctor. He was diagnosed with depression, had been seeing a psychologist, and was taking antidepressants. Although the workload and pressure of his school program were starting to get to him, he would not take time off because, as he told his father, he did not want to be a quitter.

Kevin gave no indication that he was deeply troubled. He certainly exhibited no signs of being suicidal. But on June 21, 2003, he hanged himself in his apartment. His parents say that they will never forgive themselves for failing to realize how seriously ill Kevin was. "We did not know the warning signs," says Mark Graham. "I did not know that you could die from being too sad."[71]

> "I did not know that you could die from being too sad."[71]
>
> — Mark Graham, a retired US Army major general whose twenty-one-year-old son committed suicide.

The Scourge of Stigma

Because of his personal tragedy, Graham is well aware of the link between mental illness and suicide. He acknowledges that among military service members who suffer from mental illness, stigma is an ongoing battle, a serious problem that needs to end. "No matter what rank, young soldiers, [noncommissioned officers], commissioned officers," he says, "we have got to eliminate the stigma. We've got to make sure every door our service member goes through for help is the right door with the right answer for care, and we've got to help and not judge."[72]

US Marines watch a video during a suicide prevention program at Camp Pendleton in Southern California. An alarming rise in military suicides has led to new prevention programs and efforts to convince members of the military to seek help when needed.

Yet even as military suicides have soared and the connection with mental illness has been shown, the philosophy of being tough and not showing weakness permeates all branches of the military. It is a fact that service members must be physically and emotionally strong to endure the rigors of war. But the mindset that admitting a problem and asking for help is a sign of weakness deters those who might desperately need assistance. This became apparent during a February 2013 survey by the Iraq and Afghanistan Veterans of America. When asked the top reasons for not seeking mental health care, 43 percent of respondents said they were afraid it might affect their career, and 33 percent did not want to be perceived as different by their peers.

In September 2013 a soldier shared his thoughts about the issue in an anonymous online comment:

> We have it pounded into us to be strong, never show weakness as an American Soldier in our military. . . . It is increasingly difficult to ask for help, because admitting you NEED help is a weakness. Some manage, most don't. I didn't. I was in a bad way, drinking heavily because it was the only way to get any sleep. Nightmares & flashbacks were daily. Then I hurt people without knowing what I was doing and realized I needed help. I pray my fellow soldiers will realize it is NOT weakness but STRENGTH to [seek] help.[73]

What Is Being Done?

The DoD takes the suicide problem seriously and has implemented numerous strategies to address it. One major step was the November 2011 creation of the Office of Suicide Prevention, which is charged with identifying existing suicide prevention programs, and determining how much money has been allocated for them and what needs to be done to make them work better. In a September 2013 statement, US secretary of defense Chuck Hagel emphasizes how high a priority suicide prevention is for the military. "The Department of Defense has no more important responsibility than supporting and protecting those who defend our country," says Hagel, "and that means we must do everything possible to prevent military suicide."[74]

The primary focus for the military, according to Hagel, is on mental illness and substance abuse because of their known links with suicide. Because this is such a high priority, the DoD has invested more than $100 million in research that focuses on these areas. The agency has also increased the number of mental health care providers by 35 percent, in primary care settings as well as embedded in units deployed to the front lines. Military leaders are participating in suicide prevention training, where they learn how to recognize the signs and symptoms of crisis and encourage service members to seek whatever help they need.

As for the perception that a military service member asking for help connotes weakness, Hagel emphatically refutes that. "Seeking behavioral health care is a choice that embodies moral courage,

Suicides Caused By TBI?

Military suicide has been the subject of an exhaustive amount of research, and there are many theories about its possible causes. These range from the stress of multiple deployments to undiagnosed mental illness. In May 2013 a study led by psychologist Craig J. Bryan produced another theory: concussions, which are traumatic brain injuries (TBI). Research suggests that up to 20 percent of troops deployed to Afghanistan or Iraq suffered a concussion, either from close proximity to bomb blasts or due to accidents. Studies have also revealed that a high number of military service members sustain concussions during stateside training exercises. According to Bryan's study, multiple concussions can increase the risk of suicide.

The study involved 157 military personnel and four civilian contractors who were referred to Bryan's clinic for suspected concussions while serving in Iraq. Of the 18 who had never sustained a prior concussion, none had suicidal thoughts in the previous year. Of the 58 service members who had been concussed, 3.4 percent had considered suicide during the previous year. And among those with two or more concussions, the suicide risk jumped to 12 percent. "All of a sudden the likelihood of being suicidal increased dramatically once you had the second head injury," says Bryan. Exactly how concussions might increase the risk of suicide remains poorly understood. According to Bryan, more studies are needed to determine cause and effect.

Quoted in Alan Zarembo, "Are Multiple Concussions Driving Suicides in the Military?," *Los Angeles Times*, May 16, 2013.

honor and integrity," he says. "Those values are at the foundation of what that we stand for and what we defend. . . . Always remember that our most valuable resource is each other. When one of us faces a challenge, we all must stand together. By fighting as one team, we can—and we will—help prevent suicide."[75]

General Raymond T. Odierno is a top-ranking army officer who shares Hagel's passion for helping save military service members from suicide. Because he has been with the military for more than thirty-five years, he knows that stigma often deters people who need help from reaching out for it. "The Army works against itself sometimes," he says. "We want strong, independent, mentally and physically tough people because we need that to accomplish the mission. And it gets into a bit of the stigma of coming forward and saying, well, you know, I have a little problem. . . . So you have to create an environment within your command where this becomes acceptable."[76]

For this to come about, says Odierno, the entire culture of the military has to change—which he acknowledges is a massive undertaking, but one that has already started. "We are in the beginning," he says. "If I use a football analogy, we are on about the 35-yard line and we still got quite a ways to go. . . . That said, from 2003 to now, we've come a long way with this suicide prevention. But this is a problem that's not going to end when Afghanistan is finished. This is something that's going to go on for many years afterwards. We have to be prepared to understand that."[77]

Missed Opportunities

With the military's renewed emphasis on mental health, those who study military suicide emphasize the importance of proper, thorough screening methods. Mental health screenings are a mandatory part of post-deployment health assessments, which are conducted after deployment in combat zones. These screenings are intended to detect depression, PTSD, and other mental health disorders. But according to former US Army captain Michael Cummings, the current screening process is ineffective. He says

A soldier at Fort Hood in Texas goes through a routine administrative and medical screening. Mental health screenings are now a mandatory part of post-deployment health assessments.

that service members view the questions as little more than an annoying interference with their ability to go home and get on with their lives. He explains: "Redeploying soldiers check the mental health block for a variety of reasons—to get back to drinking, to protect their careers, or to avoid more questions."[78]

Cummings himself has gone through the process several times. After his first deployment to Afghanistan he filled out the necessary paperwork and was led to a small cubicle that offered little privacy. The evaluator, who Cummings assumes was a mental health professional of some sort, referred to a checklist and asked him a series of questions about his sleep habits, whether he had bad dreams, and so forth. "Like most soldiers," says Cummings, "I wanted to finish my checklist and return to my hotel room. As soon as I finished, I would join the battalion on block leave. So I answered, honestly, 'No' to all the questions and left." Several years later, after returning from a deployment to Iraq, Cummings went to a screening session and found himself looking at the same list of questions. "I sat down with a counselor for about five minutes," he says. "Again, I answered, honestly, 'No' to all of the questions, but I couldn't believe that at a post with one of the highest suicide/discipline problems in the Army, this was all the Army had for mental health."[79]

Military officials have become aware that the current mental health screening process is not working effectively, and some have called for change. According to a study published in 2011, one solution to the problem is for screening to be conducted anonymously. The research team evaluated screening questionnaires completed by 3,502 US Army troops who were returning to Fort Stewart, Georgia, after serving a tour in Iraq. Of those service members, 1,712 agreed to complete a second anonymous survey, which they were told would be used for research purposes.

The research team analyzed and compared responses and found that reporting of depression, PTSD, and suicidal thinking, as well as of interest in receiving mental health care, was two to four times higher on the anonymous surveys compared with the routine post-deployment assessments. In the published report, the authors write: "This study indicates that the Post-Deployment Health Assessment screening process misses most soldiers with significant mental health problems. Further efforts are required to reduce the stigma of reporting and improve willingness to receive care for mental health problems."[80]

The Race to Save Lives

The US military has faced many battles over the years, and the fight to save service members from dying by their own hands is among the most formidable. The Department of Defense has put innumerable programs in place to address the problem and invested millions of dollars in research to better understand why the suicide problem exists. These and other strategies will hopefully make a positive difference in the near future so fewer lives will be needlessly lost.

Facts

- The Department of Defense reports that in 2012 the US Air Force recorded fifty-nine suicides, up 16 percent from the previous year, and the US Navy had sixty suicides, up 15 percent.

- According to the Department of Veterans Affairs, veterans over age fifty account for nearly 70 percent of all veteran suicides.

- In a February 2013 survey by the Iraq and Afghanistan Veterans of America, 30 percent of respondents said they had considered taking their own lives.

- During the summer of 2009 the Veterans Administration added a one-to-one online chat service for military veterans who prefer to reach out for assistance using the Internet.

- Department of Defense research has shown that most military suicides are committed by white men under the age of twenty-five who are in junior enlisted ranks.

- A detailed analysis released by the Pentagon in January 2013 showed that during 2011 the suicide rate for divorced military service members was 55 percent higher than for those who were married.

CHAPTER FIVE

Could Gun Control Help Reduce Suicide?

Whenever Dr. Frank Dumont looked over the day's appointment schedule and saw the name of one of his favorite patients, it made him smile. Dumont had been the man's family physician for about ten years, and when he came in for a checkup they chatted like old friends. They both lived in the Colorado mountain town of Estes Park and shared a deep love for the Rockies. They were mesmerized by the towering, majestic Longs Peak in Rocky Mountain National Park, and it invariably became the topic of discussion anytime the two were together.

Although the man was in his eighties he was physically fit, active, and enjoyed hiking the mountain trails. But then he started having problems with memory, forgetting where he put things and struggling to remember words and phrases. This was frustrating for him, and Dumont could see that he was becoming depressed. So he prescribed an antidepressant and had the man start coming in for checkups every eight weeks. During one visit Dumont asked him if he was having any thoughts of hurting himself, and without hesitation the man said no, he was not. That was the last time Dumont ever saw him. The man who had been his patient and friend ended his life by shooting himself in the head with a rifle.

Crucial Questions

Dumont was crushed to hear such dreadful news, and he was also plagued by guilt. He had purposely asked the man questions about any harmful intentions, but he had never asked about guns. He has since vowed to ask more-probing questions of patients who he knows are depressed or troubled because he does not want to lose anyone else to suicide. Dumont says that he has developed a method for asking follow-up questions that may involve asking the same things but in a different way. If he has even the slightest inkling that someone might be suicidal, he will start to push

"He Didn't Say He Was Sorry"

When Emily Frazier learned that her twenty-one-year-old husband, Ryan, had shot himself to death, she was shocked as well as grief-stricken. "Ryan had never used a gun before," she says. He had struggled with emotional issues from an incident that happened when he was a teenager, and he often had nightmares. But he was happily married, had a rewarding career, adored his young son, and was looking forward to the birth of his and Emily's second child. Then on November 21, 2008, the couple had an argument, and Ryan walked out of the house. He got in his car, drove to a nearby gas station, and bought a handgun. "I didn't realize places like that existed," says Emily.

The next morning police officers went to Emily's house and told her that Ryan had been found slumped over in his car by a construction crew. "After he died," says Emily, "I walked into the gas station where he had bought the gun, and the owner was there. I asked him about the process for selling a gun and if they ever screened people for mental illness. Then I said, 'My husband bought a gun here and shot himself.' The owner said just a couple of words. I couldn't read his emotion. I don't know if he was uninterested or shocked. He didn't say he was sorry."

Emily Frazier, "'He Was Struggling with Nightmares,'" *Guns & Suicide: The Hidden Toll*, Harvard Public Health Special Report, Spring 2013. www.hsph.harvard.edu.

the person a little more, saying something like, "So you're not really thinking about it, but have you ever thought about how you would go about it if you were going to?" Dumont adds: "I have a lower threshold for asking about a weapon in the home as well."[81]

To Matthew Miller, a physician and suicide prevention expert with the Harvard School of Public Health, Dumont sounds like a great doctor who was really looking out for his patient. "He was doing everything he could to try to keep this guy from making a suicide attempt," says Miller, "but what he didn't do was the second step, which is make it hard for him to die if he did make an attempt."[82] By making it hard for the man to die, Miller is referring to pointedly asking him if he has guns in the house or has any access to guns.

This type of candid questioning is essential, says Miller, because firearms are the most lethal of all suicide methods—90 percent of people who try to kill themselves with guns succeed in doing so. This can be compared with a drug overdose, which is fatal in less than 3 percent of cases. During questioning, if a doctor learns that no firearms are readily available, chances are good that if a patient does attempt suicide he or she will use a less lethal method. Chances are also good that the patient will survive, as Miller explains: "Instead of there being a 90-plus percent chance of death, there's a greater than 90 percent chance that they'll live."[83]

Disturbing Stats

Miller and a group of colleagues conducted a study of firearms and suicide in 2012, and the written report, published in August 2013, begins with a startling assertion: "On an average day in the United States, more than 100 Americans die by suicide; half of these suicides involve the use of firearms."[84] A CDC fact sheet, also published in 2013, shows that during 2009–2010 a total of 38,126 firearm suicides occurred among US residents, including 1,548 youth aged ten to nineteen. Since 1981, when the CDC began publishing such statistical data, firearm suicides have consistently outnumbered homicides. The gap has continued to widen through the years, though, as gun homicides have declined and suicides have not. In 2010 there were more than twice as many gun-related suicides as homicides.

According to a 2013 Harvard Public Health special report, more people in the United States kill themselves with firearms than with all other intentional means combined. This includes hanging, poisoning, overdose, jumping, or cutting. The lethality of guns is an extraordinarily important consideration because the weapons represent an irreversible solution to what is very likely a temporary crisis. In the Harvard report the authors write: "Suicidal individuals who take pills or inhale car exhaust or use razors have time to reconsider their actions or summon help. With a firearm, once the trigger is pulled, there's no turning back. . . . The method by which one attempts suicide has a great deal to do with whether one lives or dies."[85]

More people use firearms to kill themselves than any other means of committing suicide. Suicidal people who take pills or cut themselves might have time to reconsider their actions or get help, but this is usually not the case with guns.

Controversial Findings

Because firearms are the deadliest of all suicide methods, having a better understanding of the link between gun availability and suicide is a high priority for researchers. One study was led by

Eric W. Fleegler, who is an emergency medicine pediatrician at Boston Children's Hospital and an assistant professor of pediatrics at Harvard Medical School. The purpose of the study, which was published in May 2013, was to evaluate the relationship between firearm laws in the states and gun fatalities. The team analyzed data reported to the CDC from 2007 through 2010 and then compared those figures with state-level firearm legislation.

After their analysis was complete the team determined that states with the toughest gun legislation in place had a 37 percent lower rate of firearm suicide deaths compared with states that have the weakest laws. According to Fleegler, this study "speaks to the importance of having legislation." In the case of states with weak laws that are prevented from being effective because of loopholes, he says: "There are ways to make these laws better and stronger."[86]

Another emergency medicine physician, Garen Wintermute, urges caution when interpreting the study results. Wintermute, who directs the Violence Prevention Research Program at the University of California, shares his thoughts about Fleegler's study: "Correlation does not imply causation. This fundamental limitation is beyond the power of the authors to redress." Wintermute says that nearly all the links between additional laws and fewer deaths disappeared when the researchers took into account the prevalence of gun ownership in each state. "We really don't know what to do with the results," he says. "We cannot say that these laws—individually or in aggregate—drive firearm death rates up or down."[87]

Guns in the Home

Rather than focus on state firearm laws for their 2012 study, Miller's team examined the association between gun ownership and firearm suicide. Specifically, they set out to determine whether there was a correlation between guns in the home and a spike in firearm suicides, which prior studies have shown to be the case. In the published report the authors write: "Household firearm ownership has . . . consistently been found to be a strong predictor of suicide risk in studies that use individual-level data. Every US case-control study, for example, has found that the presence of a gun in the home is a risk factor for suicide."[88] To conduct the

The Gun Shop Project

Riley's Sport Shop in Hooksett, New Hampshire, sells thousands of guns each year—and is also involved with a suicide prevention group. The partnership was formed during the spring of 2009, when owner Ralph Demicco learned that three suicides, all within the same week, had been committed with guns purchased from his store. "I was devastated," he says. Demicco joined forces with mental health professionals, the New Hampshire Firearm Safety Coalition, gun dealers, and other individuals to form a unique collaboration called the Gun Shop Project. The group's purpose is to help gun stores and firing ranges learn ways to avoid selling or renting a firearm to anyone who may be suicidal.

Since the Gun Shop Project was founded, it has produced numerous materials, including instructional videos, tip sheets, posters, and brochures. As of spring 2013 about half of New Hampshire's dealers were participating. Says Demicco: "The dealers who chose not to participate, I think, in time will see the value in it." As he and his staff have become more aware of what to look for when people want to buy guns, Demicco says they have refused to sell on some occasions. Turning people away, he says, has made them "madder than hoot owls." But he believes it is his responsibility as a gun dealer to do his part to help prevent firearm suicide.

Quoted in Morgan True, "The Gun Shop Project, Suicide Prevention Campaign, Effort of Health Professionals, Gun Dealers," *Huffington Post*, April 20, 2013. www.huffingtonpost.com.

study, the team analyzed CDC suicide mortality data for all fifty US states and obtained firearm ownership information from comprehensive surveys. The same surveys also provided details about whether firearms were kept in or around the home, as well as other data relevant to the research.

At the conclusion of the study the team found that in states with high gun ownership (an average of 51 percent of adults live in households with firearms), 7,275 adults used guns to commit suicide between 2008 and 2009. This is in stark contrast with low gun ownership states (an average of 15 percent of adults in households with firearms), in which 1,697 adults committed suicide with guns. According to Miller and his colleagues, this is convincing evidence that where there are the most guns, there are also the greatest number of suicides. "Our results support the hypothesis that firearms in the home impose suicide risk above and beyond the baseline risk," they write, "and help explain why, year after year, several thousand more Americans die by suicide in states with higher than average household firearm ownership compared with states with lower than average firearm ownership."[89]

Miller is aware that not everyone is enthusiastic about this research, nor will they necessarily accept it as valid. Individuals and groups like the National Rifle Association (NRA), which is adamant about protecting Americans' Second Amendment rights, may assume that the underlying purpose was to pass laws that clamp down on individual gun ownership. But Miller says that was not the researchers' motivation. "This is not about legislating our way out of it," he says. "If I have a kid who is moody and having problems or a husband or wife who just lost a job and is being issued divorce papers, or just going through a rough time, the best thing I can do to reduce that person's immediate risk of death from suicide is to take guns out of the house."[90]

"If you look at how people get into trouble, it's usually because they're acting impulsively, they haven't thought things through. And that's just as true with suicides as it is with traffic accidents."[93]

— Matthew Miller, a physician and suicide prevention expert with the Harvard School of Public Health.

The Impulse Factor

Even if people choose to keep guns in their homes, many steps can be taken to prevent firearm suicide tragedy. Storing guns in a lockbox is one way to keep them out of reach and accessible only to the possessor of the key. Or a gun can be kept unloaded and stored in a different room from the ammunition. "The goal," says Miller, "is to put more time between the person and his ability to act. If he has to go down to the basement to get his ammunition or rummage around in his dresser for the key to the gun safe, you're injecting time and effort into the equation—maybe just a couple of minutes, but in a lot of cases that may be enough."[91]

Miller refers to this as a way of slowing down the decision-making process, which is crucial because of the element of impulsivity. Study after study has shown that most people who kill themselves act on impulse rather than plot their death ahead of time. They may have had a fleeting thought about dying but never actually planned to take their own life—and then something went wrong and they snapped. This, say the authors of the 2013 Harvard Public Health special report, dispels the myth that suicides are typically planned far in advance. "While this can be true—people who attempt suicide often face a cascade of problems—empirical evidence suggests that they act in a moment of brief but heightened vulnerability."[92]

According to Miller and his colleague David Hemenway, up to four-fifths of all suicide attempts are impulsive acts. They cite one widely quoted University of Houston study that involved 153 people between the ages of thirteen and thirty-four who had survived suicide attempts. The research team found that only 13 percent of them contemplated their suicide for eight hours or longer. Comparatively, 70 percent spent less than an hour between deciding to kill themselves and actually trying to—and for 24 percent the wait time was less than five minutes. "If you look at how people get into trouble," says Miller, "it's usually because they're acting impulsively, they haven't thought things through. And that's just as true with suicides as it is with traffic accidents."[93]

According to Linda Rosenberg, who is president and chief executive officer of the National Council for Community Behavioral Healthcare, impulsive behavior is what makes firearms a "death sentence" for people who are contemplating suicide. She has no doubt that the research is correct—people who have limited or no access to guns are far less likely to die by suicide. "Guns leave little hope for the thousands of people who survive suicide attempts

> "With a firearm, once the trigger is pulled, there's no turning back."[94]
>
> — Linda Rosenberg, president and chief executive officer of the National Council for Community Behavioral Healthcare.

every year and manage to turn around their lives," says Rosenberg. "People who swallow pills, inhale fumes, or slash their wrists have some time to reconsider their desperate actions. Even if they are not rescued, these methods often fail, leaving open the hope that they will seek treatment. But with a firearm, once the trigger is pulled, there's no turning back."[94]

Kerry Lewiecki was a young man who took his own life so suddenly, so inexplicably, that his family is certain his actions were impulsive. Lewiecki, who was twenty-seven years old, was known as an optimist, someone with a great sense of humor and a big

A breakup with a boyfriend or girlfriend, a hurtful Facebook post, or an encounter with cyberbullying leads some teens to take their own lives. Studies show that teens act impulsively in many areas, including decisions involving suicide.

laugh; someone who always had a hug ready for the people he loved. Early in the summer of 2010 Lewiecki graduated from the University of Oregon with dual degrees in law and conflict resolution. That August he planned to marry his longtime girlfriend, and invitations had been sent out for their wedding. Because Father's Day was just around the corner, he mailed a gift to his parents' home in preparation for his upcoming visit. Then, without any warning whatsoever, he purchased a gun and shot himself to death. "We had no clue he was desperate," says his father, Mike. "I don't think he'd ever shot a gun before."[95]

No one knows whether Lewiecki could have been stopped from taking his own life. But because it was obviously an impulsive move, his family cannot help thinking that something could have been done to save him. Perhaps if the law had required a waiting period for anyone who wants to buy a gun, this would have given him time to think about what he planned to do. "If it had not been so easy to buy a gun," says Mike, "maybe he would have spoken with someone or woken up the next morning and heard the birds and felt better."[96]

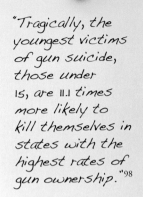

"Tragically, the youngest victims of gun suicide, those under 15, are 11.1 times more likely to kill themselves in states with the highest rates of gun ownership."[98]

— Daniel Taylor, a pediatrician with St. Christopher's Hospital for Children and an associate professor at Drexel College of Medicine.

Young Lives Blown Away

Impulsivity plays an even greater role in the suicides of young people. According to Daniel Taylor, many suicidal acts coincide with same-day crises such as a breakup with a boyfriend or girlfriend, a cell phone being taken away, a hurtful Facebook post, or taunting from bullies. Says Taylor: "A large study of completed suicides showed that more than one-third of people under 18 who took their lives had same-day crises, compared with older people, among whom fewer than one-fifth had same-day crises. This is the all-or-nothing teen brain executing at its most extreme."[97]

Taylor goes on to say that when there is a gun in the home, there is a high likelihood that it will be used by a young person in an attempted suicide. In 75 percent of cases, the guns belong to a parent. "With a 90 percent fatality rate," he says, "guns afford few second chances." He references Miller's study and offers another finding from it that relates to youth. "Tragically, the youngest victims of gun suicide, those under 15, are 11.1 times more likely to kill themselves in states with the highest rates of gun ownership."[98]

A study presented at the 2013 meeting of the Pediatric Academic Societies was conducted with children and teens who had been admitted to emergency departments (EDs). Stephen J. Teach, who is associate division chief for Emergency Medicine and Trauma Services at Children's National Medical Center in Washington, DC, explains why these locations were chosen: "For more than 1.5 million adolescents, the emergency department is their primary point of contact with the health care system, which makes the ED an important place for identifying youth at risk for suicide."[99] Study participants included 524 youth between the ages of ten and twenty-one who had been admitted for medical or psychiatric problems at one of three pediatric emergency departments. They were asked to fill out questionnaires, which the researchers then used to create screening tools. Based on the patients' responses during the screening process, the team could determine the risk factors for suicide and evaluate which youths needed further mental health evaluation.

> "Being at risk for suicide and having access to firearms is a volatile mix."[100]
>
> — Jeffrey A. Bridge, youth suicide expert at the Research Institute at Nationwide Children's Hospital and associate professor of pediatrics at Ohio State University.

By the conclusion of the study, the team had learned that there were guns in nearly 20 percent of the patients' homes. Additionally, 31 percent knew how to access the guns, 31 percent knew how to access the bullets, and 15 percent knew how to access both the guns and the bullets. Says suicide expert Jeffrey A. Bridge, another member of the research team: "This study highlights the importance of parents understanding the risks of having guns in their homes. Being at risk for suicide and having access to firearms is a volatile mix. These conversations need to take place in the ED with families of children at risk for suicide."[100]

Senseless Deaths

Health officials, physicians, mental health specialists, and researchers view suicide as an enormous problem, and this is especially true when firearms are part of the equation. Many factors come into play, most notably impulsivity and easy access to firearms. But whatever is causing the problem, those who are intimately familiar with it insist that something must be done to stop it. Says *USA Today* editor John Siniff, whose older brother shot himself to death in 2011: "We can't keep looking the other way."[101]

Facts

- Since the CDC began publishing data in 1981, gun suicides have outnumbered gun homicides.

- In January 2013 the Pentagon released an in-depth analysis showing that 60 percent of military suicides in 2011 were committed with the use of firearms that in most cases were personal weapons, not military-issued weapons.

- Federal legislation called the Brady Violence Prevention Act required a five-day waiting period for a background check before firearm purchases; since it expired in 1998, checks are now done in minutes through the Internet-enabled National Instant Check System.

- Research has shown that the risk of suicide with a gun is nearly seventeen times greater for individuals who live in a home where a firearm is kept.

- According to the Pew Research Center, by age group, people aged sixty-five and older have the highest firearm suicide rate.

Source Notes

Introduction: Preventable Tragedies

1. Quoted in Alan Duke, "'MasterChef' Runner-up Josh Marks Loses 'Battle of His Life,' Commits Suicide," CNN, October 14, 2013. www.cnn.com.
2. Quoted in Duke, "'MasterChef' Runner-up Josh Marks Loses 'Battle of His Life.'"
3. Quoted in Duke, "'MasterChef' Runner-up Josh Marks Loses 'Battle of His Life.'"
4. Quoted in Duke, "'MasterChef' Runner-up Josh Marks Loses 'Battle of His Life.'"
5. Brian Resnick, "325 Members of the Army Killed Themselves Last Year. Sorting Out Why Is No Easy Task," *National Journal*, March 7, 2013. www.nationaljournal.com.
6. Quoted in Angela Haupt, "U.S. Officials Launch New Strategy to Prevent Suicide," *U.S. News & World Report*, September 10, 2012. http://health.usnews.com.
7. National Institute of Mental Health, "The Sorrow of Suicide," *NIH News in Health*, May 2012. http://newsinhealth.nih.gov.
8. Youth Suicide Prevention Program, "Need Help?," www.yspp.org.
9. John M. McHugh, "They'll Be Glad They Lived: Action Alliance Brings New Focus to Suicide Prevention Efforts," *National Council Magazine*, 2012, p. 14.

Chapter One: How Did Suicide Prevention Become an Issue of Concern?

10. George Howe Colt, *November of the Soul: The Enigma of Suicide*. New York: Scribner, 2006, p. 291.
11. Quoted in Colt, *November of the Soul*, p. 292.
12. Quoted in Lorna Carroll, "Founder of National Save-a-Life League Visitor in St. Petersburg—Cites Many Cases in 28 Years League Has Served Humanity in Averting Suicides," *Independent*, April 19, 1934. http://news.google.com.
13. Colt, *November of the Soul*, p. 292.
14. *New York Times*, "Cities 6,509 Suicides in 6 Months of 1921," August 8, 1921.

15. *New York Times*, "Cities 6,509 Suicides in 6 Months of 1921."
16. *New York Times*, "Cities 6,509 Suicides in 6 Months of 1921."
17. Quoted in Colt, *November of the Soul*, p. 295.
18. Thomas Curwen, "Edwin S. Shneidman Dies at 91; Pioneer in the Field of Suicide Prevention," *Los Angeles Times*, May 18, 2009. www.latimes.com.
19. Edwin S. Shneidman, *A Commonsense Book of Death*. Lanham, MD: Rowman & Littlefield, 2008, p. 139.
20. Edwin S. Shneidman and Norman L. Farberow, "The Los Angeles Suicide Prevention Center: A Demonstration of Public Health Feasibilities," *American Journal of Public Health*, January 1965. www.ncbi.nlm.nih.gov.
21. Shneidman and Farberow, "The Los Angeles Suicide Prevention Center."
22. Norman L. Farberow, "Suicide Prevention: A View from the Bridge," *Community Mental Health Journal*, December 1968, p. 470.
23. Quoted in Colt, *November of the Soul*, p. 307.
24. Colt, *November of the Soul*, p. 307.
25. Colt, *November of the Soul*, p. 308.
26. US Surgeon General and National Action Alliance for Suicide Prevention, "2012 National Strategy for Suicide Prevention," September 2012. www.ncbi.nlm.nih.gov.

Chapter Two: Should More Resources Be Devoted to Mental Health?
27. Kevin Hines, *Cracked, Not Broken*. Lanham, MD: Rowman & Littlefield, 2013, p. 2.
28. Hines, *Cracked, Not Broken*, p. 57.
29. Hines, *Cracked, Not Broken*, p. 57.
30. Hines, *Cracked, Not Broken*, p. 57.
31. Hines, *Cracked, Not Broken*, p. 62.
32. Kevin Hines, "The Civil Rights Movement of Our Time," Kevin Hines Story, *Kevin's Blog*, October 23, 2013. www.kevinhinesstory.com.
33. American Foundation for Suicide Prevention, "Frequently Asked Questions," 2013. www.afsp.org.
34. Quoted in Josh Sanburn, "Inside the National Suicide Hotline: Preventing the Next Tragedy," *Time*, September 13, 2013. http://healthland.time.com.
35. Alan E. Kazdin and Sarah M. Rabbitt, "Novel Models for Delivering Mental Health Services and Reducing the Burdens of Mental Illness," *Clinical Psychological Science*, January 2013. www.sun.ac.za.

36. Quoted in Susan Donaldson James, "Suicide Prevention: 'Checking In' Can Cut Deaths in Half," *ABC News*, September 13, 2012. http://abcnews.go.com.

37. David Murphey, Brigitte Vaughn, and Megan Barry, "Access to Mental Health Care," *Adolescent Health Highlight*, Child Trends, January 2013. www.childtrends.org.

38. Substance Abuse and Mental Health Services Administration, "Sources of Payment for Mental Health Treatment for Adults." www.samhsa.gov.

39. National Alliance on Mental Illness, *Grading the States 2009*, March 2009. www.nami.org.

40. Robert Langreth and Rebecca Ruiz, "The Forgotten Patients," *Forbes*, August 26, 2010. www.forbes.com.

41. Quoted in Renee Dudley, "Study: S.C. Mental Health Cuts Highest," *Post and Courier* (Charleston, SC), November 13, 2011. www.postandcourier.com.

42. Quoted in Ilana Kowarski, "Mental Health Advocates Outraged by Lack of State Funding for Psychiatric Care, Cuts in Governor's Budget," Maryland Reporter, April 5, 2013. http://marylandreporter.com.

43. Quoted in Kowarski, "Mental Health Advocates Outraged by Lack of State Funding for Psychiatric Care, Cuts in Governor's Budget."

Chapter Three: How Effective Are Youth Suicide Prevention Efforts?

44. Quoted in Riki Parikh, "A Dialogue to Prevent Teen Suicide," Mike Johnston, blog, February 24, 2012. www.mikejohnston.org.

45. Quoted in Parikh, "A Dialogue to Prevent Teen Suicide."

46. Quoted in Parikh, "A Dialogue to Prevent Teen Suicide."

47. Quoted in Parikh, "A Dialogue to Prevent Teen Suicide."

48. Daniel Taylor, "Guns in the Home Raise the Suicide Risk for All," Philly.com, October 27, 2013. http://articles.philly.com.

49. Jane Braxton Little, "How a Small California Town Curbed a Teen Suicide Epidemic—by Talking About It," *Yes!*, November 11, 2013. www.yesmagazine.org.

50. Little, "How a Small California Town Curbed a Teen Suicide Epidemic."

51. Quoted in Little, "How a Small California Town Curbed a Teen Suicide Epidemic."

52. Quoted in Little, "How a Small California Town Curbed a Teen Suicide Epidemic."

53. Quoted in Little, "How a Small California Town Curbed a Teen Suicide Epidemic."

54. Quoted in Little, "How a Small California Town Curbed a Teen Suicide Epidemic."

55. Quoted in Brett M. Kelman, "Life Saved as an Online Mystery Is Solved," *USA Today*, May 15, 2013. www.usatoday.com.

56. Quoted in Kelman, "Life Saved as an Online Mystery Is Solved."

57. Harold Koplewicz, "Suicide and the Antidepressant Question," *Huffington Post*, March 9, 2010. www.huffingtonpost.com.

58. Quoted in Care for Your Mind, "Should We Screen Middle and High School Students for Mental Health Disorders?," October 15, 2013. http://careforyourmind.org.

59. Quoted in Rick Nauert, "Family Crisis Therapy Helps Suicidal Teens," PsychCentral, November 3, 2011. http://psychcentral.com.

60. Quoted in Nauert, "Family Crisis Therapy Helps Suicidal Teens."

Chapter Four: Should Suicide Prevention Be a Higher Priority for the Military?

61. Quoted in Michelle Linn-Gust, "Family Shares Story of Son's Tragic Death by Suicide," *Naperville (IL) Sun*, September 4, 2013. http://napervillesun.suntimes.com.

62. Quoted in Esther Bergdahl, "Military Suicide Epidemic Compels Survivor Families to Speak Out," *Medill Reports*, June 4, 2013. http://news.medill.northwestern.edu.

63. Quoted in Linn-Gust, "Family Shares Story of Son's Tragic Death by Suicide."

64. Quoted in Linn-Gust, "Family Shares Story of Son's Tragic Death by Suicide."

65. Dennis J. Reimer and Peter W. Chiarelli, "The Military's Epidemic of Suicide," Opinions, *Washington Post*, December 7, 2012. http://articles.washingtonpost.com.

66. Thomas Insel, "Where Is the Risk? What Science Tells Us About Suicide," *National Council Magazine*, 2012, p. 31.

67. Insel, "Where Is the Risk?," p. 31.

68. Insel, "Where Is the Risk?," p. 32.

69. Quoted in Jen Christensen, "Study: Mental Illness, Not Combat, Causes Soldier Suicides," CNN, August 6, 2013. www.cnn.com.

70. Cynthia A. LeardMann et al., "Risk Factors Associated with Suicide in Current and Former US Military Personnel," *JAMA*, August 7, 2013. http://s3.documentcloud.org.

71. Quoted in Michelle Tan, "Retired Two-Star Speaks Out About Son's Suicide," *Army Times*, September 25, 2012. www.armytimes.com.

72. Quoted in Tan, "Retired Two-Star Speaks Out About Son's Suicide."

73. Quoted in David Wood, "Military and Veteran Suicides Rise Despite Aggressive Prevention Efforts," *Huffington Post*, September 3, 2013. www.huffingtonpost.com.

74. Chuck Hagel, "Message from Secretary Hagel on Suicide Prevention Month," September 3, 2013. www.defense.gov.

75. Hagel, "Message from Secretary Hagel on Suicide Prevention Month."

76. Raymond T. Odierno, interview by David Wood, "Army Chief Ray Odierno Warns Military Suicides 'Not Going to End' After War Is Over," *Huffington Post*, September 25, 2013. www.huffingtonpost.com.

77. Odierno, interview by David Wood.

78. Quoted in Greg Barnes, "The Last Battle: Is the Army Doing Enough to Help Soldiers Suffering from Mental Health Problems?," *Fayetteville (NC) Observer*, September 23, 2012. http://fayobserver.com.

79. Quoted in Barnes, "The Last Battle."

80. Christopher H. Warner, George N. Appenzeller, Thomas Grieger, Slava Belenkiy, Jill Breitbach, Jessica Parker, Carolynn M. Warner, and Charles Hoge, "Importance of Anonymity to Encourage Honest Reporting in Mental Health Screening After Combat Deployment," *JAMA Psychiatry*, October 2011. http://archpsyc.jamanetwork.com.

Chapter Five: Could Gun Control Help Reduce Suicide?

81. Quoted in Eric Whitney, "How a Patient's Suicide Changed a Doctor's Approach to Guns," NPR, March 20, 2013. www.npr.org.

82. Quoted in Whitney, "How a Patient's Suicide Changed a Doctor's Approach to Guns."

83. Quoted in Whitney, "How a Patient's Suicide Changed a Doctor's Approach to Guns."

84. Matthew Miller, Catherine Barber, Richard A. White, and Deborah Azrael, "Firearms and Suicide in the United States: Is Risk Independent of Underlying Suicidal Behavior?," *American Journal of Epidemiology*, August 23, 2013, p. 1.

85. Madeline Drexler, ed., *Guns & Suicide: The Hidden Toll*, Harvard Public Health Special Report, Spring 2013. www.hsph.harvard.edu.

86. Quoted in Tom Watkins, "Study Links Gun Laws and Lower Gun Mortality," CNN, March 7, 2013. www.cnn.com.

87. Quoted in Watkins, "Study Links Gun Laws and Lower Gun Mortality."

88. Miller, Barber, White, and Azrael, "Firearms and Suicide in the United States," p. 1.

89. Miller, Barber, White, and Azrael, "Firearms and Suicide in the United States," p. 1.

90. Quoted in Carolyn Y. Johnson, "Science in Mind: Harvard Study Finds a Gun in the Home Increases Risk of Suicide," Boston.com, September 6, 2013. www.boston.com.

91. Quoted in Scott Anderson, "The Urge to End It All," *New York Times*, July 6, 2008. www.nytimes.com.

92. Drexler, *Guns & Suicide: The Hidden Toll*.

93. Quoted in Anderson, "The Urge to End It All."

94. Linda Rosenberg, "The Smoking Gun in Suicides," *National Council Magazine*, 2012, p. 6.

95. Quoted in Elizabeth Rosenthal, "Suicide, with No Warning," *New York Times*, March 10, 2013. www.nytimes.com.

96. Quoted in Rosenthal, "Suicide, with No Warning."

97. Taylor, "Guns in the Home Raise the Suicide Risk for All."

98. Taylor, "Guns in the Home Raise the Suicide Risk for All."

99. Quoted in Janice Wood, "Study Finds 1 in 5 Suicidal Teens Have Guns in Their Homes," PsychCentral, May 7, 2013. http://psych central.com.

100. Quoted in Wood, "Study Finds 1 in 5 Suicidal Teens Have Guns in Their Homes."

101. John Siniff, "The Real Gun Epidemic Is Suicides," *USA Today*, February 19, 2013. www.usatoday.com.

Related Organizations and Websites

American Association of Suicidology
5221 Wisconsin Ave. NW
Washington, DC 20015
phone: (202) 237-2280
fax: (202) 237-2282
website: www.suicidology.org

The mission of the American Association of Suicidology is to better understand and prevent suicide. Its website offers fact sheets, statistics, current research, a selection of multimedia resources, and a section devoted to survivors of suicide.

American Foundation for Suicide Prevention
120 Wall St., 22nd Floor
New York, NY 10005
phone: (212) 363-3500; toll-free: (888) 333-2377
fax: (212) 363-6237
e-mail: inquiry@afsp.org
website: www.afsp.org

The American Foundation for Suicide Prevention seeks to prevent suicide through research, education, and advocacy. Its website features a wealth of information about suicide and suicide prevention, as well as news articles, research, and public policy updates.

International Association for Suicide Prevention

National Centre for Suicide Research and Prevention
Sognsvannsveien 21, Bygg 12
N-0372 Oslo, Norway
phone: (47) 229 237 15
fax: (47) 229 239 58
e-mail: office@iasp.info
website: www.iasp.info

The International Association for Suicide Prevention seeks to prevent suicidal behavior and provide a forum for academics, mental health professionals, crisis workers, and suicide survivors. Its website features archived newsletters, a number of suicide papers, a "Groups at Risk" section, and links to resources for teens and young adults.

Jason Foundation

18 Volunteer Dr.
Hendersonville, TN 37075
phone: (615) 264-2323; toll-free: (888) 881-2323
e-mail: contact@jasonfoundation.com
website: www.jasonfoundation.com

Founded in memory of Jason Flatt, who committed suicide at the age of sixteen, the Jason Foundation seeks to prevent youth suicide through education and awareness programs. Its website offers news articles, videos, information publications, and links to other resources.

Mental Health America

2000 N. Beauregard St., 6th Floor
Alexandria, VA 22311
phone: (703) 684-7722; toll-free: (800) 969-6642
fax: (703) 684-5968
website: www.mentalhealthamerica.net

Mental Health America is dedicated to helping people live mentally healthier lives and to educating the public about mental health and mental illness. A number of articles and other publications related to suicide are available through the website search engine.

National Alliance on Mental Illness (NAMI)

3803 N. Fairfax Dr., Suite 100
Arlington, VA 22203
phone: (703) 524-7600; toll-free (800) 950-6264
fax: (703) 524-9094
website: www.nami.org

NAMI is dedicated to improving the lives of people who suffer from mental illness, as well as the lives of their families. Its website offers fact sheets, videos, online discussion groups, a special mental illness section, the *Advocate* online magazine, and a search engine that produces numerous articles about suicide.

National Institute of Mental Health (NIMH)

Science Writing, Press, and Dissemination Branch
6001 Executive Blvd., Room 8184, MSC 9663
Bethesda, MD 20892-9663
phone: (301) 443-4513; toll-free: (866) 615-6464
fax: (301) 443-4279
e-mail: nimhinfo@nih.gov
website: www.nimh.nih.gov

An agency of the US government, the NIMH is the largest scientific organization in the world specializing in mental illness research and the promotion of mental health. Its website features a special section on suicide prevention, with frequently asked questions, statistics, news articles, video clips, and a number of other resources.

Samaritans

The Upper Mill, Kingston Rd.
Ewell, Surrey KT17 2AF, UK
phone: 44 (0)20 8394 8300
fax: 44 (0)20 8394 8301
e-mail: admin@samaritans.org
website: www.samaritans.org

Based in the United Kingdom, Samaritans is a charitable organization devoted to helping people who are in crisis and having suicidal feelings. Its website offers many publications about suicide, as well as a search engine that produces numerous articles.

Society for the Prevention of Teen Suicide

PO Box 6835
Freehold, NJ 07728
phone: (973) 292-0602, ext. 3
e-mail: info@sptsnj.org
website: www.sptsnj.org

The Society for the Prevention of Teen Suicide develops and implements youth suicide prevention programs at both the state and national levels. Its website has a section containing frequently asked questions; separate sections designed for teens, parents, and educators; and links to other resources.

Substance Abuse and Mental Health Services Administration (SAMHSA)

1 Choke Cherry Rd.
Rockville, MD 20857
phone: (877) 726-4727
fax: (240) 221-4292
e-mail: samhsainfo@samhsa.hhs.gov
website: www.samhsa.gov

SAMHSA's mission is to reduce the impact of substance abuse and mental illness on America's communities. A wealth of information about mental health topics and suicide is available through alphabetized databases or the site's search engine.

Suicide Prevention Advocacy Network (SPAN)

1010 Vermont Ave. NW, Suite 408
Washington, DC 20005
phone: (202) 449-3600
fax: (202) 449-3601
e-mail: jmadigan@afsp.org
website: www.afsp.org

As the public policy arm of the American Foundation for Suicide Prevention, SPAN seeks to reduce loss of life from suicide by supporting research, educational campaigns, and policy initiatives. Its website features suicide facts, survivor stories, archived news articles, and legislative updates.

Suicide Prevention Education Alliance

29425 Chagrin Blvd., Suite 203
Cleveland OH 44122-4602
phone: (216) 464-3471
fax: (216) 464-3108
website: www.speaneohio.org

The Suicide Prevention Education Alliance seeks to prevent suicide by teaching young people to recognize warning signs and to seek professional help for themselves and others. Its website offers a number of publications and fact sheets about suicide, substance abuse, and teen depression, as well as survivor stories and links to other resources.

Youth Suicide Prevention Program

444 NE Ravenna Blvd., Suite 401
Seattle, WA 98115
phone: (206) 297-5922
fax: (206) 297-0818
e-mail: info@yspp.org
website: www.yspp.org

The Youth Suicide Prevention Program seeks to end teen suicide by increasing the public's awareness of the problem and by educating families about risk factors and effective prevention measures. The website offers news releases, statistics, frequently asked questions, and other publications related to teen suicide, along with links to additional resources.

Additional Reading

Books

John Bateson, *The Final Leap: Suicide on the Golden Gate Bridge*. Berkeley: University of California Press, 2012.

Carrie Goldman, *Bullied: What Every Parent, Teacher, and Kid Needs to Know About Ending the Cycle of Fear*. New York: HarperOne, 2012.

Jennifer Michael Hecht, *Stay: A History of Suicide and the Philosophies Against It*. New Haven, CT: Yale University Press, 2013.

Kevin Hines, *Cracked, Not Broken*. Lanham, MD: Rowman & Littlefield, 2013.

Jack Klott, *Suicide and Psychological Pain: Prevention That Works*. Eau Claire, WI: Premier, 2012.

Craig A. Miller, *This Is How It Feels: Attempting Suicide and Finding Life*. Seattle: CreateSpace, 2012.

Peggy J. Parks, *Teenage Suicide*. San Diego, CA: ReferencePoint, 2012.

Periodicals

Greg Barnes, "The Last Battle: Is the Army Doing Enough to Help Soldiers Suffering from Mental Health Problems?," *Fayetteville (NC) Observer*, September 23, 2012.

Ta-Nehisi Coates, "On Tyler Clementi's Suicide," *Atlantic*, February 1, 2012.

Tony Dokoupil, "The Suicide Epidemic," *Newsweek*, May 22, 2013.

Sabrina Rubin Erdely, "One Town's War on Gay Teens," *Rolling Stone*, February 2012.

Larissa MacFarquhar, "Last Call," *New Yorker*, June 24, 2013.

Janet Nicol, "Tears Are Good Medicine," *New Internationalist*, May 2012.

Ian Parker, "The Story of a Suicide," *New Yorker*, February 6, 2012.

Bryan Smith, "The Cluster Conundrum: Copycat Teen Deaths in Lake Forest," *Chicago Magazine*, July 2012.

Tom Smith, "Her Death Still Hurts but It Is Better Now," *National Catholic Reporter*, July 19, 2013.

Alice G. Walton, "The Gender Inequality of Suicide: Why Are Men at Such High Risk?," *Forbes*, September 2012.

Internet Sources

Centers for Disease Control and Prevention, "Suicide: Facts at a Glance," September 25, 2012. www.cdc.gov/violencepreventi on/pdf/suicide_datasheet_2012-a.pdf.

National Council for Behavioral Health, "Suicide Prevention," *National Council Magazine*, 2012. www.thenationalcouncil.org /consulting-best-practices/magazine.

Josh Sanburn, "Inside the National Suicide Hotline: Preventing the Next Tragedy," *Time*, September 13, 2013. http://health land.time.com/2013/09/13/inside-the-national-suicide-hot line-counselors-work-to-prevent-the-next-casualty.

Index

Picture Credits

AP Images: 40

© Jerry Cooke/Corbis: 15

John Gibbons/Newscom: 52

© Hill Street Studios/Blend Images/Corbis: 33

© Alec Huff/Corbis: 47

Tim Parker/Newscom: 21

© Eric Risberg/AP/Corbis: 27

The San Diego Union Tribune/Newscom: 57

© Erich Schlegel/Corbis: 61

© Ted Soqui/Corbis: 67

Thinkstock Images: 10

© Julian Winslow/Corbis: 72

About the Author

Peggy J. Parks holds a bachelor of science degree from Aquinas College in Grand Rapids, Michigan, where she graduated magna cum laude. An author who has written more than a hundred educational books on a wide variety of topics, Parks lives in Muskegon, Michigan, a town that she says inspires her writing because of its location on the shores of Lake Michigan.